In the
Footsteps
of
Robert E. Lee

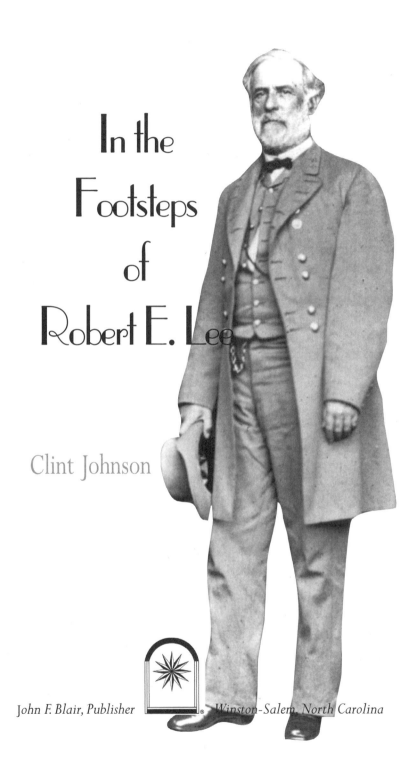

In the Footsteps of Robert E. Lee

Clint Johnson

John F. Blair, Publisher   Winston-Salem, North Carolina

Published by John F. Blair, Publisher

The paper in this book meets the guidelines
for performance and durability of the
Committee on Production Guidelines for
Book Longevity of the Council on Library Resources

Cover photographs:

Standing portrait of Gen. Robert E. Lee, by Mathew Brady, April 1865
courtesy of The National Archives
Copy print courtesy of The Museum of the Confederacy, Richmond, Virginia

From top to bottom:
White Marsh, Stuart's Hill, Stratford Hall, Grave of Traveller outside Lee Chapel
Courtesy of the author

Library of Congress Cataloging-in-Publication Data

Johnson, Clint, 1953-
    In the footsteps of Rober E. Lee / Clint Johnson.
        p.   cm.
    Includes bibliographical references (p.) and index.
    ISBN 0-89587-235-8 (alk. paper)
        1. Lee, Robert E. (Robert Edward), 1807-1870—Anecdotes. 2. Generals—
Confederate States of America—Biography—Anecdotes. 3. Lee, Robert E. (Robert
Edward), 1807-1870—Homes and haunts. 4. Historic sites—Middle Atlantic States—
Guidebooks. 5. Historic Sites—Southern States—Guidebooks. 6. United States—History—
Civil War, 1861-1865—Battlefields—Guidebooks I. Title.

E467.1.L4 J63 2001
973.7—dc21
                                                                    2001025671

Design by Debra Long Hampton   *Composition by The Roberts Group*

I dedicate this book

to two of my ancestors who fought for Marse Robert.

One was Sergeant James Madison Manley of the Eighth Florida Regiment, who lost an arm at Fredericksburg on December 11, 1862. He was standing in the open on the south bank of the Rappahannock fighting the attacking Federals while all those selfish Mississippians were hiding in Fredericksburg's houses. His wife didn't mind his war injury. They later had 13 children. The people of Fort Meade, Florida, didn't mind either. He ran a very successful bar.

The other was Captain Charles Anderson of the Sixth Georgia Regiment, who was so severely wounded at Chancellorsville that he had to resign from the Army of Northern Virginia. Anderson later became a brigadier general of Georgia militia and had the misfortune to fight one more battle—a disastrous defeat suffered at Griswoldville, Georgia, against Union general William T. Sherman's 63,000 battle-hardened veterans. The defeat must have affected Anderson's mind. He became a tax collector in Fort Valley, Georgia.

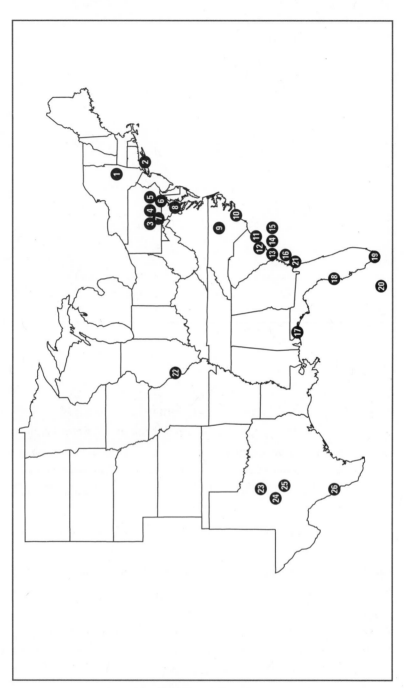

IN THE FOOTSTEPS OF ROBERT E. LEE

Eastern United States

NEWYORK

1 West Point
2 Fort Hamilton

PENNSYLVANIA

3 Chambersburg
4 Cashtown
5 Gettysburg

MARYLAND

6 Fort Carroll
7 Sharpsburg

8 WASHINGTON, D.C.

VIRGINIA

(See detailed map on page 2.)

WEST VIRGINIA

(See detailed map on page 106.)

NORTH CAROLINA

9 Warrenton
10 Fort Macon

SOUTH CAROLINA

11 Charleston
12 Coosawhatchie

GEORGIA

13 Savannah
14 Fort Jackson
15 Fort Pulaski
16 Cumberland Island

FLORIDA

17 Fort Pickens
18 Fort DeSoto
19 Fort Zachary Taylor
20 Fort Jefferson
21 Fort Clinch

MISSOURI

22 Jefferson Barracks

TEXAS

23 Camp Cooper
24 Fort Mason
25 San Antonio
26 Rio Grande City

Contents

Washington, D.C.

West Virginia

New York

Pennsylvania

Maryland

North Carolina

South Carolina

Georgia

Preface

Most Southerners—and probably many Northerners—will never forget Robert Edward Lee. Whatever else the Virginian, engineer, career soldier, general, and college president was, he remains a Southern icon.

It has become fashionable in recent years to attack heroes, particularly Southern heroes, and most particularly Lee. The attacks on Lee started with a dribble of books criticizing his military strategies and tactics, finding fault with every decision he made and blaming him for the South's losing the War Between the States. They became more intense in the last decade with Ken Burns's PBS television series *The Civil War*. Southerners knew from what angle the New Englander would approach his version of the war and of Lee when Burns casually claimed in an interview before the first episode ran that Lee was responsible for more American deaths than Tojo, the Japanese war minister in World War II. Now, even pictures of Lee are subjects of debate. Witness what happened in Richmond when a city councilman threatened to "rumble" if a mural of Lee was erected on a public wall. The mural went up, and someone firebombed it.

But Lee lives on in the hearts of people who take the time to learn about him.

On my trips to Lexington, Virginia, I've often stood back and watched the reactions of people when they gaze through the iron bars into the tomb containing the remains of the entire Lee family. You can tell that the general's crypt is the one they always look for. Some just stare, staying for several minutes in front of a simple white stone facing with a man's name on it. There is literally nothing more to see.

You can guess what they are doing. They are pondering what would have happened had "the lost order" not been found by the Federals, spoiling Lee's plan to invade Pennsylvania in September 1862 and resulting in the Battle of Sharpsburg. They are thinking through what would have happened if Lee's best general, Stonewall Jackson, had not been lost in May 1863. They are daydreaming about what would have happened had General Henry Heth not sent his division into Gettysburg too quickly on the morning of July 1, 1863, forcing Lee to fight before all his army was on the field. They are wondering what would have happened if General Dick Ewell had forced his way up Gettysburg's heights on the north side of town, as Lee had ordered him to do. All these tourists, Southerners and Northerners alike, can't help staring at the last resting place of Robert E. Lee and imagining how history might have been different.

Not many people in American history have had such power of personality and have attracted the kind of attention devoted to Lee.

This book is designed to take readers as close as possible to the historical sites associated with Lee from his birth to his death. Is it complete? Of course not. Lee was kind of like George Washington. He visited a lot of places and likely slept in many of them, but he may have stayed only one night and may have done nothing more historic than pulling down the sheet on a bed. Local historians may be disappointed—or relieved, if they don't like tourists—that I do not mention all the places where Lee set up headquarters during the war. In some cases, I likely did not know about the houses, or they are too difficult to find, or they are simply not important enough to include in a short book. I did not try to find the spots where Lee surveyed the Ohio-Michigan border, because how does one visit a border? And, since I do not think a large number of people would travel to Mexico just to see sites associated with Lee, neither did I track Lee's movements during the Mexican War of 1846-47. While the campaigns to Vera Cruz, Cerro Gordo, and Chapultepec are interesting to read about, they are difficult and expensive to trace today. For those who have the time, money, and inclination, the Mexican fort at Chapultepec is preserved as a museum in Mexico City.

In places such as Texas, Missouri, and Florida, there is little to actually see. In Texas, Lee spent most of his time in tents in the middle of nowhere. But it was there that he started worrying about what he would do if Virginia left the Union, so getting close to those sites is important to understanding Lee. Likewise, little of Lee remains in Missouri. But the Mississippi River—the lifeblood of St. Louis—is still there, and Robert E. Lee is the major reason. In a sense, the entire city of St. Louis can be considered a monument to Robert E. Lee. Mayors of the city have said so. In Florida, Lee played a minor role in inspecting the state's forts, and he spent a few nights there at the end of his life as a tourist. But just the fact that he did touristy things in the land of Mickey Mouse is fun to know.

In addition to the above, the book includes sites in most of the East Coast states from Georgia to New York. Not surprisingly, the bulk of the material concerns Virginia and West Virginia, where Lee spent most of his life and almost all of the War Between the States.

Once you use this book to reach a spot associated with Lee, look around. In some cases—like Sewell Mountain and Cheat Mountain in West Virginia—you will be looking at exactly the same thing Robert E. Lee saw. You will not see any strip malls or office buildings. You won't hear highway traffic. You won't smell factory smoke. It will be easy to put yourself back into 1861. In other spots—such as the Manassas battlefield outside Washington and Fort Hamilton in Brooklyn—going back in time will be impossible. There is too much traffic, too much city noise. But just standing where Lee stood can be rewarding. It was at Manassas where a bullet grazed Lee's cheek but did not even break his skin. It was in the Verrazano Narrows off Fort Hamilton where he pulled to safety a little dog that would later have a puppy that would become so important to him that he wrote loving letters to his wife and children describing its antics. You can read about these incidents in any number of Lee biographies, but to see where they actually happened is special.

I knew something about Lee before starting my research. But I learned much more in writing this book. One thing I learned was that the man was incredibly lucky. I found several spots in Virginia and West Virginia where Lee was almost killed or captured. On three different occasions, Union cannonballs came close to mangling him. Three times, he was almost killed or captured by Union cavalry patrols. Several times, snipers took aim at him. Every Federal missed.

I learned that Lee was a very calm man. One time, the general was drinking a glass of buttermilk in a yard when a Union cannonball zoomed by and crashed into the house. Lee didn't spill a drop. He liked his buttermilk too much. When the aforementioned bullet grazed his cheek, he didn't write his wife about it. He knew it would only worry her.

I also learned that Lee had a sense of humor, even an occasionally bawdy one. He sometimes made jokes in church, though he was a devout Episcopalian.

In short, I learned that Lee is a Southern icon whose life can still be touched by visiting the places he knew.

Acknowledgments

First and foremost, I want to thank local historians. It is the people who live in historic communities who are the key to saving old houses, old forts, old battlefields. Without local historians, history is paved over, memories are lost.

My thanks go to Robert and Nancy Buttermark, the owners of Derwent, the house where Lee lived after leaving Richmond.

Ms. Peggy Carter and Mrs. Peggy Pixley of Orlean helped me find the spot where Lee was almost captured just before Second Manassas in August 1862.

Francisco Jardin, director of the Harbor Defense Museum at Fort Hamilton in Brooklyn, showed me around the facility. He also pointed out that the Lee House on the fort, long believed to have been Lee's residence, probably was not.

Dr. Steve Grove, a historian at the United States Military Academy, directed me to the sites associated with Lee that can still be found at West Point.

For proving to me that the Internet is a wonderful research tool, I thank Jerry Nelson of Texas for helping track Lee's duty stations in that state. I also want to thank Gary Thompson, a Washington, D.C., lawyer I met on-line; Thompson checked around and found that Winfield Scott's former office is now the vice president's office.

The staff of the Missouri Historical Society sent me articles dating back more than 60 years detailing Lee's contributions toward preserving St. Louis.

Russell E. Woodburn, curator of collections at Violet Bank Museum in Colonial Heights, Virginia, took time out from his preservation work on this gem of a house museum to tell me about it.

Sture Olsson, owner of Romancoke in West Point, Virginia, showed me around his fine home, which was preserved by his parents, who moved to the house early in the 20th century.

Constance Ingalls, the owner of White Marsh in Virginia, allowed me into her home to see the parlor where Lee made some historic comments. As a bonus, she also showed me a more recent (but just as precious) artifact—a thank-you letter from Douglas Southall Freeman, author of the four-volume biography of Lee. Freeman visited her house back in the 1940s.

Art and Carol Bergeron of Chester, Virginia, made some suggestions on where to find important Lee sites around Petersburg.

The staff at the Carlyle House in Arlington told me about the hotel that used to stand nearby.

The volunteers at the Manassas battlefield showed me around Stuart's Hill.

I want to thank Bill Boyd, one of my reenacting compatriots from the 26th North Carolina Regiment, who has traveled with me on research trips on two different books. I hope he continues to come along to help read maps and keep me company on future research ventures. He is the type of man who looks harmless enough that two very nice ladies in Orlean, Virginia, invited us out of a thunderstorm and helped us find a very unusual historic spot—the most important wide spot in the road in the entire state of Virginia, where Lee was almost captured.

I also want to thank the staff of John F. Blair, Publisher, in Winston-Salem, North Carolina, the publisher of my first three books, for understanding the value of a book that lets people see today what Robert E. Lee saw in his day.

Finally, I want to thank my wife of 17 years, Barbara, for allowing me to buy just one more Civil War book, just one more reenacting uniform, just one more statue, just one more musket (four so far), just one more cap-and-ball pistol (two so far). Likewise, I appreciate her willingness to stop at just one more museum, tramp around just one more battlefield, and wander around just one more cemetery looking for just one more Civil War grave. She is proud of herself now that she can tell the same Civil War stories that I have been telling at book signings and slide shows.

VIRGINIA

Smith Island

This Chesapeake Bay island, split between Virginia and Maryland, is accessible by ferry from the end of US 360 at Reedville, Virginia. The ferry runs from May through October; call 804-453-3430 for information.

While it may be hard to think of Robert E. Lee as an economic developer, environmentalist, landlord, and beachcomber, he did occasionally play those roles when he married into the wealthy Custis family in 1831, just two years after graduating from the United States Military Academy.

In 1832, while stationed at Fort Monroe, Virginia, Second Lieutenant Lee made a business trip to Smith Island, a barrier island that had been in the family of his father-in-law, George Washington Parke Custis, since 1691. Mr. Custis asked Lee to visit the island to determine what sort of value could be derived from it. Today, Smith Island caters to fishermen and tourists. In 1832, it was the Custis family's

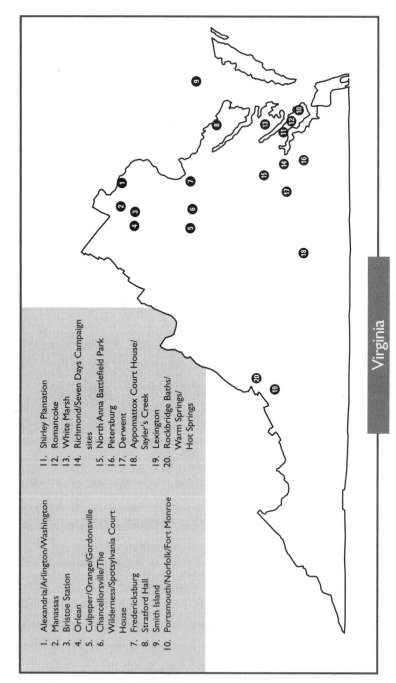

Virginia

1. Alexandria/Arlington/Washington
2. Manassas
3. Bristoe Station
4. Orlean
5. Culpeper/Orange/Gordonsville
6. Chancellorsville/The Wilderness/Spotsylvania Court House
7. Fredericksburg
8. Stratford Hall
9. Smith Island
10. Portsmouth/Norfolk/Fort Monroe
11. Shirley Plantation
12. Romancoke
13. White Marsh
14. Richmond/Seven Days Campaign sites
15. North Anna Battlefield Park
16. Petersburg
17. Derwent
18. Appomattox Court House/Sayler's Creek
19. Lexington
20. Rockbridge Baths/Warm Springs/Hot Springs

IN THE FOOTSTEPS OF ROBERT E. LEE

most remote holding, located 13 miles out in Chesapeake Bay from the Northern Neck of Virginia and the southern shore of Maryland opposite Smith Point, Virginia, on the mainland.

In a letter to his father-in-law after his visit, Lee described the island as having good soil in its glades and being thick with timber in some places. He suggested that the timber be harvested and sold on the mainland to builders of ships and homes. Thanks to his engineering training, he also noticed that beach erosion was a problem. He wrote how part of the island was "wearing away, the beach which used to protect the glades has been in many places leveled, and the water at common high tide finds its way into the glades and renders the pasturage not so good." There were four tenant farmers on the island assigned to take care of small herds of cattle and sheep. Lee suggested that the herd of cows be thinned and the sheep sheared. He also visited the keepers of a government-owned lighthouse. Lee remarked in his letter on the remarkable variety of seafood and seabird eggs he ate while a guest of the lonely lighthouse keepers. Lee's stay on the island was not entirely pleasant. He complained about "moschettoes" and the "quantity of ticks (of which I got full)." He also tossed one of the tenants off the island for being a habitual drunk.

Lee apparently never returned after his one visit.

Stratford Hall

Lee's birthplace is on CR 214 near the Potomac River, just off VA 3 about 42 miles east of Fredericksburg. The house and grounds are open to the public daily except for Thanksgiving, Christmas, and New Year's. For information, call 804-493-8038 or visit www.stratfordhall.org.

Stratford Hall, the birthplace of Robert E. Lee

Robert Edward Lee, a man who spent more than 35 years in military service, never owned a home of his own. From his birth in 1807 to his death in 1870, he slept in his parents' homes, in barracks, in post family housing, under the stars, in a military tent, in his wife's inherited house, and in many homes borrowed from individuals both during and after the war. But he never purchased a home with his own money.

Yet there was one house that stayed on Lee's mind to the end of his days. It was the place of his birth—Stratford Hall in Westmoreland County, Virginia.

At Christmas in 1861, when his wife, Mary, was still mourning the loss of Arlington, her family's home, to Union occupiers, Lee wrote her a note: "It is vain to think of it [Arlington] in a habitable condition. It is better to make up our minds to a general loss, but they cannot take away the remembrance of the spot. I wish I could purchase Stratford. That is the only place I could go to, now accessible to us, that would inspire me with feelings of pleasure and local love. It is a poor place, but we could make enough cornbread and bacon for our support and the girls could weave us clothes. I wonder if it is for sale and at how much."

Sometime after the war, a family friend sent Lee a photograph of

Stratford Hall. "Your picture vividly recalls scenes of my earliest recollections and happiest days. Though unseen for years, every feature of the house is familiar to me," Lee wrote in thanks.

Thomas Lee, a brother of Robert's great-great-grandfather, started construction on Stratford Hall sometime in the 1730s, after he bought the land on which the house stands from a great-great-grandfather of George Washington. The location—a hill overlooking the Potomac—was selected for more than its excellent view. In those days, the river was the highway of colonial Virginia. Thomas Lee wanted to see what types of ships were moving up and down the river, particularly if they were flying the skull and crossbones, as pirate ships were beginning to make pests of themselves in Tidewater Virginia.

Historians are unsure who designed Stratford Hall, which is characterized by its broad, sweeping, exterior staircases leading up to the front and rear doors and its eight massive chimneys serving 16 fireplaces on the main floor and in the basement. It is assumed that the architect must have modeled it after a house in England. It may have been designed to honor the home of Richard Lee (grandfather of Thomas) in the village of Stratford Langton in Sussex County, England. Built of bricks manufactured from clay on-site and timber cut from the surrounding forest, Stratford Hall was likely the most magnificent private dwelling in Virginia—and probably in all the colonies—when it was finished.

The home passed down to Lee sons and daughters through the generations. General Henry "Light Horse Harry" Lee and Ann Hill Carter Lee, Robert's parents, moved into Stratford Hall after their marriage in 1793. Or, more accurately, Mrs. Lee did. Lee, who acquired his military nickname by his adroit handling of cavalry during the American Revolution, actually spent little time at the house or with his wife. Instead of improving and farming the land surrounding the plantation and securing the future for his wife and children, he spent his time on various schemes of buying and selling land—and in chasing other women, a bad habit he had for much of his life. It did not go unnoticed by the woman who loved him despite his many failings.

Robert, the third of the Lee sons, was born on January 19, 1807, in the master bedroom on the southeast side of the house. He was placed in a crib that is still in the room. Family tradition says this was the same room in which two cousin Lees, Richard Henry Lee and Francis Lightfoot Lee—both signers of the Declaration of Independence—were also born. However, some historians think those cousins were born before the house was finished.

Though the house was opulent, the Lee family's life was not. Just 16 months after Robert's birth, his half-brother Henry inherited the house as a means of keeping it out of the hands of his father's creditors. Two years after Robert's birth, Light Horse Harry was arrested for nonpayment of debts and briefly put in jail. It was after this incident that Mrs. Lee decided she would no longer live in Stratford Hall and depend on the kindness of her stepson. The house was much too big, much too isolated, and much too filled with memories of her husband's inability to love her and his children.

When Robert was just over three years old, the family left here for the last time to move to Alexandria, 90 miles away, where they had relatives. The guides at Stratford Hall and some Lee biographers tell a story that one of the last things the toddler Robert did before leaving the house was to say good-bye to the angels in the nursery— actually, angels embossed on the irons in the fireplace. More than 50 years later, Lee remembered that his mother planted a horse chestnut tree in the garden of the house before their carriage pulled away.

He never again lived at Stratford Hall, though he did visit on occasion.

Fredericksburg viewed from Chatham Hall

Fredericksburg

Fredericksburg is located just off I-95 about midway between Washington, D.C., and Richmond. Visitors may also reach the town via US 1, US 17, and VA 3. Chatham Manor, operated by the National Park Service, is on the north bank of the Rappahannock River off VA 3 just across from downtown Fredericksburg. A small fee is charged that also covers the Fredericksburg and Chancellorsville battlefields; call 540-654-5121 for information. Two of the principal Lee sites associated with the Battle of Fredericksburg are Lee Hill and Hamilton's Crossing. Lee Hill is reached by turning on to Lee Drive just west of the intersection of US 1 Business and VA 3. Hamilton's Crossing, Lee's headquarters site along the railroad, is located near the end of the National Park Service road.

Chatham Manor sits just across the Rappahannock River from Fredericksburg on property first explored by John Smith in 1608.

Lee Hill, where the general watched the Battle of Fredericksburg unfold

The house, built by William Fitzhugh, the maternal grandfather of the future Mrs. Lee, was finished in 1771. There are two legends of how and where Lee proposed to Mary. One says that, in the summer of 1830, it was in the west yard of this house that the 23-year-old lieutenant brought up the subject of marriage to his childhood friend and distant cousin, 22-year-old Mary Anna Randolph Custis. The story says Lee proposed to Mary under a large tree that he would look for through binoculars during the Battle of Fredericksburg in December 1862, when he was on Lee Hill about two miles southwest of here.

Fredericksburg's battle sites lie across the river to the south of the main part of town. It was from the top of what is now called Lee Hill that the general watched the Battle of Fredericksburg unfold between December 11 and December 13, 1862. Lee made this hill a temporary battlefield headquarters. His more permanent headquarters were at Hamilton's Crossing on the railroad at the end of Lee Drive, about two miles away.

This part of the battlefield turned out to be the exact center of the fight. To Lee's left was Marye's Heights, under the command of General James Longstreet; Marye's Heights was the focus of the Union army attacking through the streets of downtown Fredericksburg. To his right was the flatter part of the line, under the command of General

Thomas J. "Stonewall" Jackson, who would face an even larger Federal force. There were far fewer trees on the Lee Hill in 1862 than there are today, so Lee had a clear view of what was happening on either side of the line.

At his headquarters at Hamilton's Crossing, Lee developed his strategy of allowing the Federals under General Ambrose Burnside to cross the Rappahannock. He put the strategy into effect from Lee Hill, his hilltop headquarters. Lee's plan was simple—allow the Federals to think that they were accomplishing something by overcoming the stiff resistance put up by a brigade of Mississippians and three companies of the Eighth Florida Regiment posted in downtown Fredericksburg. But what Burnside had not thought about was that once the Federal army was across the river, the soldiers would be forced to march uphill into the face of Lee's entrenched army. Longstreet confidently proclaimed that Marye's Heights was so well defended that, given enough ammunition, he could kill every man in the entire Union army before one of them could get close enough to even touch the now-famous Stone Wall. Longstreet's artillery chief confidently proclaimed that his guns were placed so that "not even a chicken" could survive on the field.

From Lee Hill on the afternoon of December 11, 1862, the general rode back and forth along his lines, making sure there were no gaps and that the men were digging trenches. On at least two occasions, he crept forward in front of his right flank to observe the size of the Federal force. Once, Jackson went with him. It was Jackson's aide, Prussian Heros von Borcke, who finally convinced the two generals that they were much too close when they could distinguish individual Federals digging entrenchments. On another occasion, Stuart accompanied Lee on a foray to the right flank. This time, Lee got close enough to hear the voices of the Federals. It was not until the scouting party came under fire from some Federal sharpshooters that Lee was persuaded to retire.

On the morning of December 12, Lee watched the Federal army

Artillery on display at Lee Hill

from this hill. Since the leaves were off the trees and most of the battlefield south of the town had been cleared for use as cattle pasture, Lee and the rest of the Southerners could easily keep track of the depredations committed against the town. Looting was rampant. Precious food and furniture were pulled from houses, piled in the streets, and burned in acts of pure maliciousness, rather than from military necessity. It was not the first time the Federals had warred against Southern civilians, but it was the first time they had done so in front of the South's most successful general. While Lee had not shown himself inclined toward revenge in any battle so far, it was not a good idea on the part of the Federals to destroy the town in which he had become engaged to his beloved wife.

On the morning of December 13, the Federal attack finally began just as expected, through the town and up Marye's Heights, the main thrust coming against Jackson's right flank. From Lee Hill, Lee watched as wave after wave of Federals fell in front of the Stone Wall on the left flank. A more disturbing sight lay to his right. He watched as a Federal division disappeared into the woods, moving toward his lines. But within minutes, he saw the same division rushing back toward the river in full retreat, Rebel-yelling Confederates in hot pursuit. Lee turned to Longstreet and said one of his most famous statements, overheard and recorded by a British correspondent. Seeing Jackson's

Confederates chasing the Federals, Lee said, "It is well that war is so terrible [or] we should grow too fond of it," meaning that only the gore of war can overcome the pure pleasure of watching brave men carry out a battle plan and their duty.

Lee's strategy of forcing Burnside to attack his entrenched army worked. Neither of the Federal flank attacks broke the Confederate line. Lee ordered his men to dig in even deeper on the night of the 13th, as he waited on the hill for another attack the following day. He believed—probably rightly—that if Burnside made one more series of attacks, the Army of the Potomac could literally be destroyed. "My army is much stronger for these new entrenchments, as if I had received reenforcements of 20,000 men," Lee said.

The attack Lee hoped for never came. During the night of December 13, Burnside's generals convinced him that further attacks against the heights would be fruitless. By the morning of December 16, Burnside's army was back on the north side of the Potomac. Lee later revealed in letters written at Hamilton's Crossing that he was upset that the Federal army had been able to slip back without being dealt a crushing blow. "We had really accomplished nothing; we had not gained a foot of ground, and I knew the enemy could easily replace the men he had lost," he wrote.

Lee Hill was not a safe place for the general to have his headquarters. Pay particular attention to the 30-pounder Parrott rifled cannon

Monument on the railroad at Hamilton's Crossing

on display. Lee had only two of this type of long-range cannon at Fredericksburg. During the battle, both of them blew up. One of them sent showers of fragments within feet of Lee, Longstreet, and the army's artillery chief, General William Pendleton. Amazingly, no one—not even the cannon's crew—was injured by the explosion. In addition, a Federal shell buried itself in the ground near where Lee was standing. The shell did not explode.

The other Fredericksburg site closely tied to Lee is Hamilton's Crossing. It was about a mile north of that headquarters site along the railroad that Major John Pelham, a 23-year-old Alabaman, rapidly moved his two cannons around the battlefield to slow the entire Federal assault. Watching from Lee Hill, Lee remarked, "It is glorious to see such courage in one so young!"

It was at Hamilton's Crossing that Lee showed his sharp, if rarely displayed, sense of humor. Several days after the battle, a local citizen came bearing a gift for the general—a large jug of the type that normally held wine or homemade whiskey. Lee called to his generals, asking them if they cared for "a glass of something." Smacking their lips, the generals gathered around as Lee's mess steward pulled the cork and poured them all glasses of buttermilk.

It was also at Hamilton's Crossing that Lee acquired his wartime pet—not a dog or a cat, but a hen. A local family had sent the general several chickens, intending that they be slaughtered. One, however, made its way into Lee's tent and laid an egg under his cot. By proving her value, the hen thus saved her own life. She spent her days walking around in front of Lee's tent, apparently safe in the knowledge that as long as she kept laying eggs and stayed around men familiar with her, she would not end up in a common soldier's stew pot.

Whenever Lee's headquarters were subsequently moved, Bryan, the kitchen steward, picked the chicken up and loaded her on top of the headquarters tent wagon. The hen traveled with Lee to every battlefield. She even delayed the retreat from Gettysburg briefly when she was nowhere to be found. She was finally discovered already perched in her spot in the wagon, apparently having flown there on her own. She, too, was ready to leave the scene of the devastating defeat.

The hen—whose name, if she had one, has been lost to history—survived nearly two years. Bryan finally cooked her at Orange Court House, Virginia, in 1864, when he found he had nothing else to serve the general and an unnamed distinguished guest.

Chancellorsville/The Wilderness/ Spotsylvania Court House

These three major battles were fought on virtually the same ground. Chancellorsville lies about 12 miles west of Fredericksburg via VA 3. The Wilderness is another six miles west, also on VA 3. Spotsylvania is about five miles south of Chancellorsville and the Wilderness; access is via VA 208 (Courthouse Road) from the east or CR 613 (Brock Road) from the northwest. Today, all three battle sites are administered by Fredericksburg and Spotsylvania National Military Park. Call 540-373-6122 for information.

In 1863 and 1864, Lee fought three battles in an area barely 10 miles square. The first, Chancellorsville, established him in the eyes of his countrymen—both North and South—as a military genius. The second, the Wilderness, was Lee's first meeting with a Union general who refused to leave a battlefield even though beaten—U. S. Grant. The third, Spotsylvania Court House, forced Lee to face the reality that Grant would slowly grind the Army of Northern Virginia into the ground.

Robert E. Lee and Stonewall Jackson had their last council of war here on May 1, 1863.

Chancellorsville, fought over four days, started on May 1, 1863, when Union general Joseph Hooker crossed the Rappahannock River about 10 miles west of Lee's army, which had spent the winter in Fredericksburg. Faced with 75,000 Union troops moving on his left flank and another 40,000 stationary in front of him, Lee split his army. He left 10,000 in Fredericksburg and took 50,000 with him to face Hooker, who was advancing toward a wayside inn that sounded like a town: Chancellorsville.

When the advance forces of Lee's army under Stonewall Jackson neared Hooker, the Union general did a curious thing: he pulled back in a partial retreat. Hooker's subordinate generals, suspecting they outnumbered Lee, pleaded with Hooker to attack, but he refused. He wanted to see what Lee would do.

As the sun set on May 1, Lee and Jackson, sitting around a campfire less than a mile from the Federal lines, pondered how to "get at those people," as Lee put it. Lee's cavalry general, J. E. B. Stuart, rode up with news that gave Lee an idea. Stuart had discovered that the Federal right flank was not anchored to anything defensible, such as a riverbank or trenches. In fact, the far right of Hooker's army was in an open camp with hardly any pickets on duty.

With that valuable information, Lee split the army once again the next day, Jackson taking his entire corps of 28,000 men on a 14-mile march on a wide arc around and toward the Union flank. To the Federals, it looked like Jackson was retreating toward Richmond. What the Federals perched in trees could not see was that once the Confederate line dipped out of sight down a road, it made a hard right turn on to a little-used country road that angled west, not south, the apparent line of march. Jackson's march took virtually all day, while Lee stayed behind with barely 15,000 men to face 50,000 Federals. Had Hooker ordered even one exploratory charge, he would have discovered the Confederate lines to be hollow. One charge might have captured Lee himself. But Hooker was content to wait.

As dusk settled in on May 2, Jackson drew his men up in a two-mile line in the woods a few hundred yards west of the Federal right flank. When all his regimental colonels reported they were ready, Jackson turned to General Robert Rodes and gave a simple order: "You may send your men forward."

The Federals' first hint that anything was wrong came when frightened deer and rabbits started running through the 11th Corps' camp. Right behind them came thousands of Confederates. The Federal resistance collapsed so quickly that Jackson's men pursued too fast. Order began to fall apart as regiments lost track of each other in the gathering darkness. Jackson and his staff rode forward between the lines to see if the Federals were still running or were setting up defensive positions. He then turned around and was returning to his own lines when a nervous Confederate regiment, unaware that their commander was riding patrol, fired into the riders coming from the direction of the Federal lines. Jackson was severely wounded in the shoulder and hand. Lee learned late on May 2 that Jackson was wounded but had no time to see to him personally.

On May 3, with J. E. B. Stuart filling in for Jackson, Lee attacked

Hooker again. Hooker pulled back to the river. Lee then learned that the Federals in Fredericksburg had overrun his positions and were now on their way to attack him. Caught between Hooker on his front and John Sedgewick coming in on his right, Lee split his army yet again, sending a small portion toward Salem Church, about four miles west of Fredericksburg. The Confederates won that battle, too. Having lost two battles in as many days, Hooker pulled back across the river, leaving the field to the Confederates and inadvertently creating the image of Lee as invincible.

Lee returned to virtually the same battleground on May 5, 1864, when U. S. Grant crossed the Rapidan River and entered the Wilderness, a tangled shrub forest that even the locals avoided because it was almost impenetrable. Knowing that whoever controlled the two roads through the Wilderness controlled the battle, Lee sent his corps straight down the roads, effectively creating two battles simultaneously, separated by a couple of miles of undergrowth. That night, the woods caught on fire, burning hundreds of wounded men to death.

On May 6, the exhausted Third Corps of A. P. Hill was being pushed down the road by the superior forces of Union general Winfield Scott Hancock. Lee threw himself into the fight, briefly walking his horse toward the onrushing Federals before a handful of Texans forced him to turn around and leave the battlefield.

In the end, the Wilderness was a draw, both sides suffering mightily but neither striking the other a killing blow. What was different about this battle was that every other Union general who fought against Lee had retreated once the battle was over. Grant turned his horse in the same direction Lee's army had taken.

The very next day, the Battle of Spotsylvania Court House began about five miles south of the Wilderness. Lee's army raced ahead of Grant and dug in on some high ground within minutes of the arrival of the lead elements of the Federal army.

For the next two weeks—from May 7 through May 19—Grant's army sent attacks almost daily against Lee's dug-in men in what was likely the most horrible fighting of the war. Dead and wounded men, mostly Federals, lay between the lines for nearly two weeks in the sun, the rain, and the mud. One battle lasted more than 20 hours.

Spotsylvania Court House was similar to Fredericksburg in that Lee's men were in defensive positions for the entire battle, waiting in trenches for the Federals to attack them. What Lee learned at Spotsylvania was that Grant did not mind losing a great number of men. Every other Union general had been timid about making frontal assaults against Lee. Grant was a different sort of man.

Finally, after fruitlessly trying to force Lee from his trenches, Grant pulled back, not in retreat but in a flanking maneuver south toward Richmond. Lee had to pull out of his trenches and head south, too, in order to protect the Confederate capital. From May 1864 until April 1865, U. S. Grant would control the conduct of the war in Virginia.

Visitors should pay the admission fee at the Chancellorsville or Fredericksburg visitor centers before touring the three battle sites.

At the intersection of VA 3 and CR 610 less than a mile east of the Chancellorsville Battlefield Visitor Center is the foundation of the Chancellor Inn. It was here after the Battle of Chancellorsville that Lee's men engaged in a loud cheer for their general. Hearing that cheer and looking at his men after one of the hardest fights of the war, Lee decided that it was almost time to carry the war into the North for the second time. (The first such attempt was in September 1862, resulting in the Battle of Sharpsburg.)

A sublime geographic spot lies about a mile south of the Chancellorsville Inn site at the intersection of CR 610 and Furnace Road. It was here on the night of May 1, 1863, that Robert E. Lee and Thomas Jonathan "Stonewall" Jackson had their last council of war, sitting on two boxes pulled around a campfire. The spot is marked by historical signs.

This was not a safe place to have a field headquarters. On at least one occasion when it was still daylight, a Union sharpshooter perched in a tree fired on the two generals. They merely moved out of sight and continued trying to find a means to dislodge the Federals, whose front was only a few hundred yards away.

That night, the two generals discovered a way. Confederate cavalry had observed that the Federal right flank was "in the air," meaning that it was not anchored to any natural defense such as a river or manmade defense such as a trench line. The Union's 11th Corps, on the far right, was camped in a leisurely fashion, as if they were well behind their own lines. Lee suggested that Jackson might find a way to attack that flank. Jackson conferred with some locals, who recommended using two roads that would shield Jackson's movements.

Jackson surprised Lee for the last time sitting around this campsite. When Lee asked how many troops he would carry with him on his flank march, this reply came back: "My whole corps." Lee, who would be left with fewer than 15,000 men, did not flinch. He allowed Jackson to take his corps.

The next morning before dawn, the two generals conferred at this campsite. No one was close enough to record the conversation. Jackson was mounted. Lee was standing on the ground. They exchanged a few words, and Jackson pointed down Furnace Road. Lee nodded. The two would never see each other again. The next night, Lee was sleeping here when he heard someone talking. After inquiring what was happening, he learned of Jackson's wounding.

Lee visited the abandoned Federal artillery position at Hazel Grove, which lies on Stuart Drive northwest of the campsite. Though Lee stayed near his headquarters during many battles, he seems to have moved all over the field at Chancellorsville, keeping in constant contact with his generals.

The principal Lee site in the Wilderness is the Widow Tapp Farm, located on CR 621 (Orange Plank Road); turn south off VA 3 on to CR 621 at the west end of the Chancellorsville property and drive about three and a half miles. It will be necessary to park in a small lot west of the Widow Tapp Farm and walk back to the markers describing the action here. Note the small stone marker right next to the road.

It was here at the Widow Tapp Farm that a handful of Federal skirmishers missed their chance to kill Lee, A. P. Hill and J. E. B. Stuart. Early on May 5, 1864, the three generals were talking about tactics when they looked up to see a line of Federal skirmishers coming out of the woods at them just yards away. Incredibly, as soon as they appeared, the Federals melted back into the woods, almost as if they were embarrassed to have disturbed the high-ranking Confederates. According to reports, there was nothing to stop them from shooting at the generals. All three were dismounted and apparently without any close detachments of soldiers to protect them.

The next day, May 6, brought one of the most dramatic moments of Lee's life. He was watching helplessly as Hill's corps came streaming past him in retreat on this road, fleeing advancing Federals. He was mounted on Traveller beside some cannons firing up the road at the Federals. At that moment, out of the corner of his eye, Lee noticed men marching toward the enemy.

"Who are you, my boys?" he cried.

"Texas boys!" they shouted in reply. They were the advance guard of Longstreet's long-awaited corps, which had not yet been in the fighting.

"Hurrah for Texas!" Lee cried. His staff must have looked at each other. General Lee rarely showed that sort of emotion.

As the Texans started to march forward, they noticed Lee riding with them. They instantly knew he intended to go into battle with them. They stopped and turned Traveller around. "Lee to the rear!" they shouted.

Lee tried to resist them. Finally, a stern-looking, huge sergeant grabbed Traveller's reins and turned the horse around. The sergeant was forcibly taking Lee to the rear when Longstreet appeared and Lee snapped out of his trance.

The Texans marched into oblivion. More than 800 moved forward from this point. Fewer than 200 were left alive or unwounded 20 minutes later.

A marker at the Widow Tapp Farm indicates where the Texas troops forced Lee to the rear at the Wilderness.

When Lee rode up to him, Longstreet joked about the precarious position the commanding general was in, with the Federals advancing down the road. Longstreet said if Lee wanted to lead the attack, he was welcome to do so, and Longstreet himself would go to a safer place. Lee got the message and joined his staff officers farther away from the whining bullets.

Lee again showed his willingness to lead an attack just a week later at Spotsylania Court House. CR 613 (Brock Road) leads southeast for about eight miles from the Wilderness to the Spotsylvania battlefield. Take the battlefield tour road and make the first stop at the western end of the Mule Shoe battlefield. Note the spot where a 20-inch tree was felled by minie balls. Lee himself came to see this gruesome tourist attraction—a large tree cut to the ground by lead flying through the air.

Continue around the battlefield road. Pull over near the end at the site of the McCoull House. A historic marker is on the spot. During the height of the Battle of the Mule Shoe, Lee discovered his line collapsing. Soldiers began streaming to the rear, abandoning the trenches. Lee could not stop them. Within a few minutes, he ran into General John Gordon, a Georgian commanding men from his own state and Virginia. Without orders, Gordon was massing his two brigades to fill the breach that had been opened. He was ordering his regiments into place when he noticed Lee on Traveller staring toward the approaching Federals. At that moment, Gordon's own coat was pierced by a bullet, indicating that they were well within range of the Federal muskets. Gordon shouted at Lee, "These Georgians and Virginians have never failed you. They will drive the enemy back. Go back, General Lee!"

Men from the brigades took up the shout. Yet another sergeant—this one from a Virginia regiment—grabbed Traveller's reins and led the horse to the rear. Gordon's men indeed stemmed the Federal tide, just as the Texans had done earlier.

Lee's headquarters were about 400 yards behind the McCoull House.

One Lee site—Spotsylvania's courthouse itself—lies on CR 208 (Courthouse Road) a couple of miles south of the battlefield property. Somewhere near where the courthouse stands, Lee experienced a very close call. He had Traveller's instincts to thank for saving both their lives.

The site where a 20-inch tree was felled by minie balls during the battle at Spotsylvania Court House.

Near the site of the McCoull House, Lee was forced to the rear by his troops during the Battle of the Mule Shoe.

Lee again was far forward from where he should have been and well within range of both Union artillery and muskets. He had just quieted a rearing Traveller and all seemed calm when Traveller suddenly reared again. Just at that instant, a solid shot from a Union cannon passed underneath the horse. Had Traveller not reared, taking Lee up and backward, the general would have likely been smashed.

Once again, for the third time in just over a week, Lee's men started shouting at him to get to the rear, where he belonged.

"I wish I knew where my place was on the battlefield. Where ever I go someone tells me that is not the place for me to be," Lee complained to his staff with a hint of humor.

Both the Lee and Washington families worshiped at Christ Episcopal Church.

Alexandria

The city is located south of Arlington and just across the Potomac River from Washington, D.C. The downtown area is accessible off I-395; follow the signs for Old Town Alexandria, the core of the city. The principal Lee sites— including Christ Episcopal Church and the future general's boyhood home—are concentrated in an area encompassing about 15 blocks, principally along Washington and Fairfax Streets.

Robert went to what would now be called elementary school at the Alexandria Academy, located on the east side of Washington Street between Duke and Wolfe Streets. It was here under the watchful eye of teacher William Leary that Lee first showed the talent for mathematics that would serve him well in his early career as a United States Army engineer. Lee would never forget his old teacher. In fact, Leary visited Lee in Lexington nearly 47 years later, in 1869, at which time

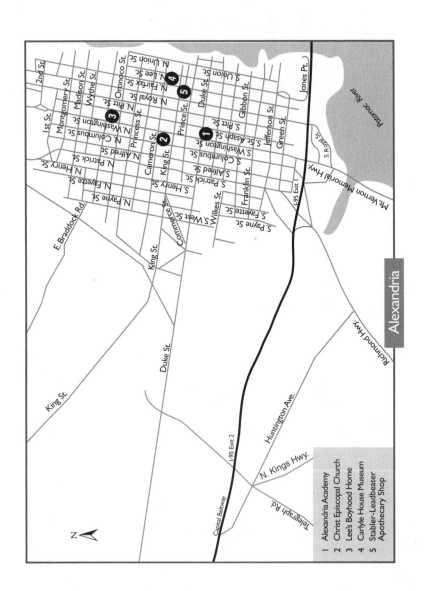

Alexandria

1 Alexandria Academy
2 Christ Episcopal Church
3 Lee's Boyhood Home
4 Carlyle House Museum
5 Stabler-Leadbeater Apothecary Shop

Pew #46, where Lee usually sat, is located at the left front of the church.

Lee expressed his appreciation for the "affectionate fidelity which characterized your teaching and conduct towards me." Lee, then in his 60s, offered to write a letter of recommendation attesting that the elderly Leary was still a good teacher. That letter returned the favor Leary had done for Lee in writing a letter that helped him obtain an appointment to West Point in 1825.

Christ Episcopal Church lies about three blocks north, at the southwest corner of Washington and Cameron Streets. Completed in 1773, this church is doubly historic, as both the Lee and Washington families worshiped here. Lee attended Christ Church regularly from the time he was a child, though he was never confirmed until after the death of his beloved mother-in-law, Mary Lee Fitzhugh Custis. In the summer of 1853, at the age of 46, apparently to seek solace from the grief he felt at losing a woman he considered his second mother, Lee formally joined the church with two of his daughters.

It was on the steps of Christ Church on April 21, 1861, that Lee learned he would be named general in command of all of Virginia's forces. He had come to church that day to worship and

*Lee lived in this home from the age of 10
through 17.*

to pray that just such an occurrence would not happen.

The pew where Lee usually sat (number 46) is located at the left front of the church; it is marked, and visitors can sit in it. There is a small historical display about the old church in the modern church next door, including a mention of how Union soldiers stole some items from the church. Among the items still missing are the chalice and the original George Washington nameplate from his pew. The church asks descendants of those Union soldiers to return the items should they ever be discovered in the family possessions. Tours of Christ Episcopal are conducted weekdays and Sundays; call 703-549-1450 for details.

The Lee family's first home in Alexandria was on the north side of Cameron Street just two houses east of the intersection with Washington, diagonally across the intersection from Christ Church. The house, now an office building, is not open to the public, but it does have a historical marker on it.

Three blocks north and half a block east of Christ Church is what is known as the Boyhood Home of Robert E. Lee, at 607 Oronoco Street. In 1816, the Lee family moved to this home, which was located directly across from the townhouse of the Fitzhugh family, relatives of Lee's mother. Lee lived here from age 10 through 17. It was from here that he left for West Point, after getting a coveted appointment from President James Monroe. Actually, the home was historic even before Lee became famous. The Marquis de Lafayette visited Robert's widowed mother here in 1824 to thank her for Light Horse Harry's service. Even earlier, the house had hosted the marriage of George Washington Parke Custis (the step-grandson of George Washington) and Mary Lee Fitzhugh, the parents of Robert's wife, Mary.

The house was once a museum and may become one again, though it is currently in private hands and is closed to the public.

At 609 Oronoco (actually part of the same building) was the Hallowell School, which Robert attended as a type of prep school in anticipation of taking the entrance exams for West Point. Like William Leary, teacher Benjamin Hallowell was impressed with Robert's comprehension of the complicated mathematics that would serve him well in the future as an engineer.

It is three and a half blocks east and three blocks south to the Carlyle House Museum, located at the southeast corner of Fairfax and Cameron Streets. In front of the museum once stood Green's Mansion House, a hotel where Lee held a public audience in May 1869. The "shadow" of the hotel can be seen on the building next door to where the hotel stood. Estimates are that several thousand people filed past the general to pay their respects. He did not seem to mind, as he knew many of them. "There is no community to which my affections more strongly cling than that of Alexandria, composed of my earliest and oldest friends, my kind school-fellows, and faithful neighbors," Lee said. Among the throng were some former slaves from Arlington.

A block and a half farther south is the Stabler-Leadbeater Apothecary Shop, at 105 South Fairfax Street. The shop operated from 1792 until 1933. Famous Virginians from Washington to Lee patronized it. One legend has Lee picking up some medicine in the shop when he was first informed about John Brown's raid in October 1859. He may have heard about the raid in the shop, but most historians place Lee at home in Arlington, several miles away, when he got his official orders to rush to Harpers Ferry.

One incident that can be traced to the apothecary occurred on the morning of April 19, 1861, when Lee was in Alexandria to pay his bill. He saw a newspaper headline proclaiming that the state's general assembly had voted to secede. The druggist asked Lee what he thought of the legislature's action. "I must say I am one of those dull creatures that cannot see the good of secession," Lee said, a subtle dig at the Deep South "fire eaters" who for the past five months had been calling for the Southern states to leave the Union.

One Alexandria-area house that was dear to Lee was Ravensworth, a Fitzhugh home. The house burned down years ago and is now the site of a shopping mall on Braddock Road.

Arlington

Arlington is the name of a county, a city, a National Cemetery, a plantation, and a famous home. The city is located about seven miles north of Alexandria and across the Memorial Bridge from Washington, D.C. The National Cemetery and the home are accessible off the George Washington Parkway. Admission is free; call 703-695-3250 for information.

Now the most famous cemetery in the country, Arlington was once a plantation that was in the Custis family for nearly 70 years. Mrs. Lee inherited the plantation upon the death of her father, George Washington Parke Custis, in 1857. Managing the plantation and sorting out his dead father-in-law's tangled business affairs was such a massive job that Lee took a leave of absence from the army for more than two years.

Abandoned by the Lees early in 1861, since it was just across the

General Montgomery Meigs personally supervised the burial of twenty-six bodies in Mrs. Lee's rose garden as a signal to the Lees that they would never again have use of Arlington.

Potomac River from the Federal army, Arlington was purchased by the Union government for nonpayment of taxes. It was first used by the army as a military outpost to protect Washington. But by 1864, the government was running out of space to bury the still-growing number of Union soldiers who were dying in northern Virginia.

The quartermaster general of the army, General Montgomery Meigs, a Georgian by birth who openly expressed hatred for all Southerners who had left the army for the Confederacy, was given the task of finding land for a new cemetery. Meigs did not even conduct a formal search for land suitable for a military cemetery. Rather, he ordered the grounds of Arlington to be made ready to accept the bodies of soldiers. What made the order particularly galling to Lee was that he and Meigs had once been friends. They had served together while diverting the course of the Mississippi River at St. Louis in 1836.

When Meigs visited the house two months after his order creating the cemetery, he was furious to discover that the burial parties were putting the new graves far from the house. He ordered 26 new bodies to be brought immediately across the Potomac from the hospitals in Washington. He personally supervised their burial in Mrs. Lee's

General Montgomery Meigs, who was given the task of finding land for a new cemetery, is one of seventy-nine Civil War generals buried at Arlington National Cemetery.

rose garden. Even if the South won the war, Meigs meant to make sure that the Lees would never again have use of their magnificent house.

Seventy-nine Civil War generals are buried at Arlington National Cemetery, including two Confederates. The most unusual monument in the cemetery may be the Confederate Memorial, located 400 yards west of the Tomb of the Unknown Soldier. Erected in 1915 by the United Daughters of the Confederacy, the bronze statue gives a defense of the Confederate cause by the allegorical use of bronze figures representing the South.

The imposing mansion lies on top of the hill. Construction on Arlington started in 1802. It was the dream home of Custis, the adopted grandson of George Washington. It took workers 14 years to complete the home, recognized as the most impressive house on the Potomac River.

When Custis and his wife, Molly, learned that a distant cousin of theirs, Robert E. Lee, had asked their only daughter, Mary, to marry him, they were less than thrilled. While military service was an acceptable profession, the Custis family was well aware that Lee had

The imposing mansion at Arlington lies on top of a hill.

been forced into a career as an army officer because he had no money or other means of educating himself. Lee had no land, no inheritance, and no prospects other than the monthly pay of an officer in the service of a country at peace. By contrast, the Custis family was at the top of the social ladder. They were linked by blood to George Washington, practically a saint in the United States of the 1830s.

That she would marry below her social status mattered not at all to Mary. Just as Lee never considered another woman for his wife, Mary never considered another man for her husband. She had loved Robert since they were children playing on the Arlington estate. Through the tangled web of intermarriage among Virginia's top families, Lee and Mary were distant cousins and had known each other virtually all their lives.

There are two legends about where Lee asked Mary to marry him. One places the moment at Chatham Manor in Fredericksburg, while the two were strolling on the lawn. Another places it at Arlington, when Mary was getting Robert a piece of cake while he was visiting. On June 30, 1831, Robert and Mary were married in the parlor of Arlington. It was a marriage that lasted to their deaths and saw the birth of four daughters and three sons. It was a happy, strong marriage, though somewhat sad, as Mary was often sick and in pain from rheumatoid arthritis. Even during her youth, she found it difficult to walk. While living at Arlington as an adult, she often had to use a wheelchair. Mary's failing health did not diminish Robert's love for her. Though he enjoyed the company of attractive women, he always looked upon them as conversation partners. No hint of infidelity on Lee's part brought about by Mary's infirmities has ever surfaced.

Starting in 1831 and lasting through 1861, Lee lived in this house or visited when on leave from duty stations as far away as Georgia and New York. Mary lived on base at Fort Monroe, but she and the children remained at Arlington during Lee's service in the Mexican War and part of his service in New York.

Before entering the house, touch the knocker on the front door. It was likely this same knocker that a young United States Army lieutenant named James Ewell Brown Stuart used to alert Lieutenant Colonel Lee that he was needed immediately at the War Department in Washington in October 1859. From there, Lee went to Harpers Ferry to put down John Brown's slave rebellion. Two years later, J. E. B. Stuart joined the Confederate army and began his rise through the ranks to become famous as Lee's cavalry chief.

The parlor, the first room on the right from the entrance, is where Robert and Mary were married. It is furnished with many pieces of Lee furniture or facsimiles and arranged as it was when the house was in its splendor.

In a hallway leading to a room housing some large paintings by George Washington Parke Custis are some furniture pieces covered in red upholstery that Lee acquired when he was superintendent of cadets at West Point in the 1850s.

On the second floor in the master bedroom is perhaps the most famous desk chair in the South. On the night of April 19, 1861, Lee stayed up all night pacing the floor and agonizing over a question only he could answer. Should he resign from the United States Army and join his beloved Virginia in leaving the Union? He signed his resignation letter to the secretary of the army while sitting in this chair. He also wrote a much more detailed, apologetic, and friendly letter to Winfield Scott. "Save in defense of my native State, I never desire again to draw my sword," Lee ended his letter. After attending Christ Church in Alexandria on April 21, he left for Richmond on April 22 to take command of Virginia's troops.

There are some amusing stories associated with so sad a place as Arlington.

When Lee returned from the Mexican War in 1847, the first member of the household to recognize him riding up the winding road to the house was not his wife and children, but Spec. Spec was a black-and-tan terrier born to a dog Lee had rescued by pulling her from the water of the Verrazano Narrows off Fort Hamilton, New York. Spec's act had precedence in Greek mythology. When Ulysses finally returned after years away from home performing his tasks, only his dog recognized him.

That family reunion at Arlington also proved embarrassing to both father and namesake son. Lee hugged and kissed Mary and each of their children, starting with the oldest. When it came time to sweep up the youngest, Robert Jr., Lee called out, "Where is my little boy?" The soldier then reached down and grabbed up a four-year-old with a head of golden curls. Unfortunately, it was not Robert Jr. It was a visiting friend. "I remember nothing more of any circumstances connected with that time, save that I was shocked and humiliated. I have no doubt that he was at once informed of his mistake and made ample amends to me," wrote Robert Jr. in his memoirs.

The Lee family lived at Arlington from 1857 to 1861 following the death of Custis. It was from 1857 to 1859 that Lee took his absence from the army to bring the plantation back from shabby disrepair. It took hard work with very little money, but Lee's ability to manage funds and a labor force—skills he would soon need in his military command—resulted in a comeback for Arlington.

One thing Lee refused to do was sell any of the estate's slaves to raise cash. Instead, he honored to the letter Custis's request that the slaves be freed within five years of his death. Lee took time out from fighting the Civil War in 1862 to sign papers freeing all the slaves on the plantation. One of those slaves, Selina, is credited with preserving many of the George Washington artifacts at Arlington. She gathered them up and then demanded an audience with the commanding Union general, at which she persuaded him to protect the artifacts by moving them to the United States Patent Office.

Robert E. Lee never returned to the house, though he did visit Alexandria and Washington, D.C., after the war. There is no record that he ever saw what had been done to the house and the grounds he had so lovingly restored.

Mrs. Lee, however, did visit one time not long after the war. Her carriage pulled to the front portico. One of her former slaves recognized her and brought her a drink of water. Mrs. Lee, an invalid by that point, did not get down from the carriage. She thanked the woman for the water and left, never to see her house again.

MANASSAS AREA

Orlean

This village lies about 10 miles northwest of Warrenton and 30 miles west of Manassas on CR 688 (Leeds Manor Road) north of US 211.

Lee and Longstreet stopped in Orlean on the night of August 26, 1862, and were prepared to eat their own rations when they received an invitation to dine at the house of the Marshall family. The home, called Edgewood, still stands about three-quarters of a

Lee and Longstreet dined at Edgewood on their way to Manassas Junction.

mile north of "downtown" Orlean on the left side of Leeds Manor Road. It is marked by a sign.

The Confederates used Leeds Manor Road to get to the Second Manassas battlefield. Jackson's corps had already used it to get behind Union general John Pope's lines. Not long afterwards, Lee, Longstreet, and the main body of the Army of Northern Virginia followed in anticipation of catching Pope in a pincer movement that would crush his army and possibly end the war with a march on Washington.

Lee was never closer to being captured or killed than he was late that month, when on one day he and his little staff of clerks and secretaries faced down an entire Federal cavalry regiment and the next day he shrugged off a bullet graze from a Federal sharpshooter, who missed killing the war's most successful general by a fraction of an inch.

Glenaire (Vermont)

This home is located southwest of the junction of CR 647 and CR 635 about 4.5 miles north of Orlean.

The intersection where Lee and Longstreet were almost captured by Federal cavalry.

The fine two-story home called Glenaire (known during the war as Vermont) stands at the intersection that may have been the most important wide spot in the road in the Civil War.

At dawn on August 27, 1862, Mrs. Marshall fixed breakfast for her famous guests. Feeling well fed and confident that they could beat Pope, Lee and Longstreet rode off that morning in very good moods—so good, in fact, that they forgot simple security measures. The two, one a general in command and the other a corps commander, rode at the heads of their columns. In other words, the most important men in the Army of Northern Virginia were acting virtually as scouts for the entire army. Apparently, no one suggested that they should ride in the middle of the column in the event they ran into an unexpected Federal patrol.

The two generals and their staffs did exactly that. Just west of this intersection, a lone scout came rushing back to Lee and Longstreet with the cry, "The Federal cavalry is upon you!"

Lee and Longstreet obediently lined up behind their staffs, who were armed only with pistols. The Federals, the Ninth New York Cavalry, apparently took only a glance at the tightly packed line of a half-dozen staff officers and wrongly concluded that they were facing a full cavalry regiment equal to their own. The New Yorkers turned around and rode away as fast as they could. What is amazing about their action is that the incident took place in midmorning daylight, hours after dawn had broken. The Federals should have noted how thin the little line of staff officers was. They probably could have even seen the two generals behind the lines, if they had taken the time to assess the situation before turning and fleeing.

The encounter was more than a close call. It could have been the end of Confederate successes in Virginia. What would have happened if Lee and Longstreet had been killed or captured? Would they have been exchanged if captured? Would Jackson have been named the new general of the Army of Northern Virginia? Would there have been any Confederate successes such as Fredericksburg or Chancellorsville had Lee not been around to direct them?

Lee and Longstreet did not know what to make of the Federal cavalry. Was Pope closer than they imagined? Was it a lone patrol, or was it part of a larger force? Lee could not even send any cavalry after the Federals to determine where they were headed, as he had given all his cavalry to Jackson.

After that scare, Lee encountered the lady who owned Vermont. She was sitting in a carriage that no longer had horses. They had been stolen by the Federals. She had hitched her carriage and gone down to the road in hopes of seeing Lee. She joked with the general that losing two horses was a heavy price to pay just to see him.

There is an interesting coincidence about this incident at Vermont. Lee would meet the Ninth New York Cavalry again. They were in Buford's cavalry brigade, which held up Lee on the first day of Gettysburg. In fact, a member of the Ninth New York fired the first shot at Gettysburg.

Manassas National Battlefield

Manassas lies about 20 miles west of Alexandria. Visitors can reach the National Battlefield by exiting I-66 on to VA 234 North. It is about a mile to the visitor center and another half-mile to the junction with US 29. By turning left on US 29 and driving about two and a half miles, guests can visit Stuart's Hill, the site of Lee's headquarters during the opening of Second Manassas. A fee is charged at the National Battlefield; for information, call 703-361-1339.

The Battle of Second Manassas, fought on August 29 and 30, 1862, came about because of a captured order. When Lee observed that Union general John Pope had carelessly boxed in his army on two sides by putting it between the Rappahannock and Rapidan Rivers, he decided to try to bottle up the Federals on a third side by using his cavalry, then sweep in from the fourth side with his infantry to crush them. He wrote out an order to his cavalry describing the plan for them to form the third side, but that order was captured. A suddenly observant Pope pulled his army out of danger.

Still anxious to get at Pope, Lee split his army and ordered Jackson's corps around Pope's flank and into his rear. Moving at lightning speed, Jackson was able to capture tons of Federal supplies at Manassas Junction almost before Pope realized he was even on the move. Unaware that Lee's army was in two pieces, Pope moved his entire force northward to retake Manassas Junction, thus giving Lee the opportunity to catch him in a pincer movement.

Pope, a general Lee called a "miscreant" for his harsh treatment of Southern civilians, never seemed to grasp what was happening on the field in front of him. Jackson was able to open the battle by ambushing

Stuart's Hill, the site of Lee's headquarters during the opening of Second Manassas

an entire Federal column moving down the Warrenton Turnpike (today's US 29). For the rest of the battle, Pope threw various divisions into the fray, but he never organized an overwhelming attack on Jackson's position in an unfinished railroad cut. That was lucky for Jackson, since his men were easily outnumbered and could not have sustained a large attack.

During the day, Longstreet's corps reached the field. His men concealed themselves so well that Pope refused to believe that Confederate reenforcements had arrived. Pope repeatedly ordered Fitz John Porter to attack what he thought was a weak Confederate right flank, but Porter, knowing Longstreet was in front of him, refused.

On the night of August 29, Jackson and Longstreet drew their lines closer together. The next day, Pope, seeing empty trenches in front of him, thought the Confederates had left the field. He ordered Porter to pursue what he assumed was a fleeing Confederate army. Porter reluctantly followed the order and sent his men into a firestorm. Jackson's troops fired so much that they ran out of ammunition and were forced to throw rocks at the Federals.

Just as the Federals were retreating, Longstreet, who Pope still refused to believe was on the field, launched a counterattack on the Federal left wing. Tens of thousands of fresh Confederates swept the field of exhausted Federals. Only a last-ditch defense set up on Henry

House Hill (the scene of the climax of the Battle of First Manassas, fought in July 1861) kept the Union army from being totally smashed and opening the way for Lee to advance on Washington.

Visitors to Stuart's Hill should note that this is the site where the so-called Third Battle of Manassas was fought several years ago, when a developer threatened to level the hill in order to put in a shopping center. The National Park Service was able to buy the hill at a tremendous profit to the developer and make it part of Manassas National Battlefield.

It was on or near this hill that Lee experienced the closest call of his entire life. As he arrived on the field, he rode forward to see what was happening. Within minutes, he returned to his staff and calmly told them that a Union sharpshooter had just missed him. His staff examined him and found a very slight red mark on his cheek. The sniper's ball had not even broken the skin. Lee never mentioned the incident to his wife in his letters home. In fact, only one of his staff officers made mention of it, and then only in his postwar book. Even in those days before television news, officers knew that newspaper accounts of the near death of Lee would give a boost to the North and depress the South.

After Longstreet's attack on the Federal left flank sent thousands of Federals scurrying to the rear, Lee, ignoring the pleas of his staff to stay in the rear, rode to his most forward battery. As he was looking through his binoculars at the still-close enemy, one of his staff told him that a young gunner wanted to say something to him.

"Well, my man, what can I do for you?" Lee asked.

"Why, general, don't you know me?" the gunner asked.

Under the grime of powder from the cannon was his youngest son, Robert Jr.

On August 31, the battle was over and rain was falling. So much rain was coming down, in fact, that it threatened to impede Lee's goal of pursuing Pope and cutting him off from Washington. That morning, Lee donned rubber overalls and a poncho and set out to see how bad the roads were. While riding together, he and Jackson developed the idea of Jackson's rushing ahead to try to cut off Pope, which would result the next day in the Battle of Chantilly.

That afternoon, Lee dismounted near the Stephens Farm, east of the National Battlefield property and closer to Washington. Suddenly, a cry went out: "Yankee cavalry!" It was exactly the same cry Lee had heard just a few days before on the road to Manassas. He lunged toward Traveller to grab the reins in the event he would need to mount quickly. He tripped on his overalls and fell, stopping himself from hitting heavily by putting both hands out.

Those 55-year-old hands were fragile. Lee broke a small bone in one hand and badly sprained the other. Both had to be put into splints. The pain was so intense that Lee could no longer mount Traveller. He had to ride in an ambulance for several days and was still in pain during the Maryland campaign. It would not be until mid-October that Lee would be able to dress himself or even sign his name.

That was the bad news. The good news was that in the course of less than two months, Lee's Army of Northern Virginia had won two different battles (Seven Days and Second Manassas) against two different generals (McClellan and Pope). In the coming four months, he would defeat another two armies at Sharpsburg and Fredericksburg and a third general (Burnside). Second Manassas set the stage for Lee's invasions of the North. The Richmond press that had demeaned him at the start of 1862 was praising him in the middle of the year.

Bristoe Station

The site where this battle was fought is private land. Much of it has been developed, so there are few vantage points from which visitors can get a feel for what happened here on October 14, 1863. The best place is the intersection of the railroad and CR 619 (Bristow Road) about a half-mile southeast of VA 28, approximately five miles southwest of Manassas.

There is not much to see at Bristoe (or Bristow) Station today. And thanks to the ever-advancing commercial and residential development pushing outward from Washington and Manassas, there may be nothing to see in the future. Battlefields in this part of Virginia are in constant threat of disappearing under housing developments and shopping malls.

But it was here at Bristoe Station that Robert E. Lee experienced one of the saddest scenes of his military career. It was here that several hundred of Lee's best soldiers were killed because their commander, A. P. Hill, one of Lee's most trusted generals, failed them miserably.

In October 1863, George Meade's Army of the Potomac, which had been advancing on Lee in the Mine Run Campaign to the south, was now retreating back north along the Orange & Alexandria Railroad line. The Confederates—Hill's Third Corps leading the way—discovered they were gaining on the Federals when they started to find campfires still burning.

As Hill arrived in this area from the west, he saw hundreds of Federals retreating across Broad Run to the north. He ordered two brigades to rush north after the fleeing Federals, hoping he could capture them and their precious equipment and food.

While Hill's desire to capture the enemy was good, his execution of the plan was deeply flawed. He did not order any scouting of what was on the southeast side of the steep railroad embankment that those two brigades would be passing. The Union's Second Corps was hiding behind a long mound of dirt. Rising as one, the Federals sent a sheet of deadly fire down the flanks of the Confederates. The fire was so concentrated that whole lines of Confederates fell dead in perfectly straight lines. In a battle that lasted less than 40 minutes, the Confederates lost 1,300 men killed and wounded.

The following day, October 15, Lee rode alone with Hill to a low hill in the area of this intersection. Many of the Confederates still lay where they had fallen on the field. Hill tried to explain why he had forgotten to scout the embankment before ordering his men forward, but Lee raised his hand to silence him. In one simple sentence, Lee acknowledged that his subordinate had made a terrible mistake but made it clear that the army had no time to punish him. "General, bury these poor men and let us say no more about it," Lee said.

Those men still lie under the fields in unmarked graves, waiting for developers' bulldozers to run over them.

Ellington/North Anna Battlefield Park

The private home known as Ellington is about 30 miles north of Richmond. Pointed out by historical markers, it is on the west side of US 1 near the bridge over the North Anna River, about two miles north of CR 684. North Anna Battlefield Park, maintained by Hanover County, is on CR 684 about two and a half miles off US 1. The park is open during daylight hours; call 804-365-4695 for details.

It was at Ellington, while watching his men defend the North Anna, that Lee experienced one of his many close calls. The owner of the house recognized Lee and offered him a glass of buttermilk, Lee's favorite beverage. As Lee was drinking it, a Union solid-shot cannon-ball hit the ground, caromed past him, and embedded itself in the front-door frame. Lee barely flinched. He thanked the homeowner for his kindness and handed back his glass without even making a comment on the cannonball. Lee would later regret stopping for that drink of buttermilk.

Travelers wanting to think about Robert E. Lee the strategist can pick no better place than nearby North Anna Battlefield Park. Chances are that they will find themselves alone at this quiet, off-the-beaten-path battlefield offering two miles of trails. Here, Lee and the Army of Northern Virginia had their last real chance of splitting up and de-feating Grant's Army of the Potomac.

When the Federals pulled away from the disastrous two weeks of heavy fighting in mid-May 1864 at Spotsylvania Court House, it did not mean that Grant was giving up. It just meant that he was looking for another place to engage Lee as the Federals slowly pushed toward Richmond. Grant's strategy was different from that of previous Union generals. All the generals preceding him had set Richmond as an objective for capture. Grant, on the other hand, reasoned that Richmond was not an object that needed capturing, but that Lee's army was an object that needed destroying. He decided to keep pushing toward Richmond as a means of keeping Lee close to him, so he could attack again.

Lee kept falling back toward Richmond, keeping Grant in front of him. It was here on the North Anna that he saw a chance to hit Grant hard again. The idea was for Lee's army to fall back to the south side of the little river (not even 30 yards wide), destroy the bridges over it, and force Grant to attack across the water and up toward the heights on the south side.

In one regard, it was a smaller version of Lee's successful defense against Burnside at Fredericksburg in December 1862. But there were some significant differences. Lee's men had been fighting for a full month and were at the point of exhaustion. And there were far fewer of them than there had been 18 months earlier. The Federals, on the other hand, were only growing stronger each day with fresh soldiers coming into the army.

Lee formed his army into a **V** shape, the sharp tip of the **V** pointing at the shallowest section of the river. The Confederates repulsed one Federal attack at this point. Upriver, however, the Federals forced their way across against A. P. Hill's men, leading Lee to make one of his rare public outbursts at Hill: "Why can't you be like Jackson?"

In one sense, Hill's failure to hold the Federals was a lucky break, as Lee quickly came to realize. When Lee got his scouting reports, he learned that the Federals were now broken up into three parts, thanks to the meandering nature of the North Anna. He realized that if he could quickly bring his entire army to bear on each separate part of Grant's army, he could chop it up piece by piece. The river would keep one part from rushing to the rescue of any other part.

Lee's strategy fell apart when he fell apart. It was at his headquarters tent in these woods that he became violently ill with a stomach disorder—probably food poisoning from the buttermilk he had drunk only a short time earlier.

Lee was so ill on May 25 that he never left his tent. His staff worried that the physical stress he was suffering might aggravate his heart problems. All Lee could do was moan in frustration, "We must strike Grant a blow! We must never let him pass us again!"

Yet strangely, Lee never issued any order to strike that blow. Though he had corps commanders A. P. Hill and Richard Anderson (who had taken over Longstreet's corps after his wounding at the Wilderness), Lee didn't direct them to attack the split-up segments of Grant's army.

After one stupendous failure at attacking the **V**—an attack that was not authorized by Grant—the Federals pulled back. Finally seeing the problems the North Anna posed him, Grant pulled both of the separated pieces of his army on the south side of the river back to the north side. The big battle Lee hoped to fight at the North Anna never materialized.

It took several days for Lee to get over his stomach problems. By the time he did, Grant was on the move again to the southeast, heading slowly but surely toward Richmond. Lee likely knew that Grant's true objective was his army, but he also understood that every future battle would be in defense of Richmond.

Why didn't Lee turn over his command here when he was unable to direct the battle himself? Historians speculate that he simply did not have the confidence in Hill and Anderson that he once had in Jackson and Stuart, both now dead, and Longstreet, now severely wounded. Could Hill and Anderson have defeated Grant on their own, while their chief was sick on his cot? Perhaps, but Lee had seen Hill and Anderson fail on separate occasions. Both corps commanders had proven themselves good fighting generals, but they were not adept at planning strategy.

This park has excellent trenches, so well preserved that visitors can easily see regimental breaks, as shown by digging styles. Some commanders would order their men to dig deeper than others. The trenches also feature rarely seen traverses, meaning that the trenches were filled in so that they could be defended from the side if the enemy outflanked the defenders and captured part of the trench line. Lee was a strong believer in trenches dating back nearly 20 years to the Mexican War. Trenches had kept his men alive on battlefields for the last three years, and they kept his men safe here on the North Anna. These preserved trenches provide a testament to Lee's skill in fighting a defensive battle.

Richmond

I-95 and I-64 are the major access routes to the city. Several Lee sites are concentrated in about a 15-block area in downtown Richmond. The Dabbs House is at the eastern edge of downtown, on Nine Mile Road just east of Exit 193 off I-64. Chickahominy Bluffs Battlefield Park is east of the city off Mechanicsville Turnpike (US 360).

No city symbolizes Lee more strongly than Richmond, though he lived here less than four months when he arrived at the start of the war in 1861 and then another three months after the war in 1865. He spent a few nights in Richmond during the war when visiting President Davis, but he never occupied a house here. He found the city too big for his tastes. But if Lee had not successfully defended Richmond from General George McClellan coming up the Peninsula in June 1862, from General Ambrose Burnside coming down from Fredericksburg in December 1862, and from General U. S. Grant coming overland in 1864, the war probably would have ended earlier with the symbolic capture of the Southern capital. Lee and Richmond will always be linked.

One of the must-see Lee sites in downtown Richmond is the Museum of the Confederacy, located at Clay and 12th Streets. The building houses a number of the general's artifacts, including a tent that he used, his familiar broad-brimmed hat, his gloves, his eating utensils, and his headquarters flag, a modification of the First National Flag with the stars arranged in an **A** shape. The museum is open daily; call 804-649-1861 for details.

The White House of the Confederacy is next to the museum. Lee frequently met here with President Jefferson Davis and other war

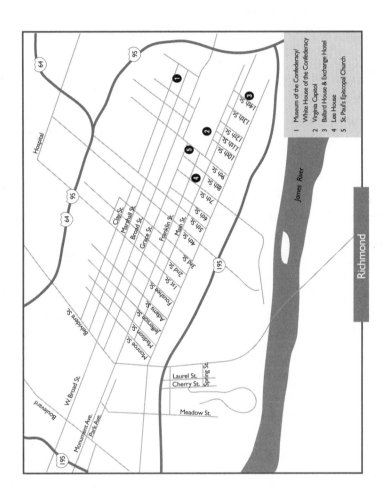

Richmond

James River

1 Museum of the Confederacy/
  White House of the Confederacy
2 Virginia Capitol
3 Ballard House & Exchange Hotel
4 Lee House
5 St. Paul's Episcopal Church

Hospital

64
95
64
95
95
195
195

14th St.
13th St.
12th St.
11th St.
10th St.
9th St.
8th St.
7th St.
6th St.
5th St.
4th St.
3rd St.
2nd St.
1st St.

Clay St.
Marshall St.
Broad St.
Grace St.
Franklin St.
Main St.

Foushee St.
Adams St.
Jefferson St.
Madison St.
Monroe St.

Belvidere St.
W. Broad St.
Monument Ave.
Park Ave.
Boulevard

Laurel St.
Cherry St.
Spring St.
Meadow St.

Lee frequently met Jefferson Davis and other war strategists at the White House of the Confederacy.

strategists. How secure those meetings were is still up for debate. A slave servant in the White House of the Confederacy has long been suspected of memorizing what she heard and what papers she managed to read, then passing the information along through a spy network. Visiting the White House requires a separate ticket, which may be purchased at the Museum of the Confederacy.

Early in the war, Lee met with Vice President Alexander Stephens in the Bruce House, located on the northwest corner of Clay and 12th across from the White House of the Confederacy.

Many of the Richmond buildings Lee frequented have either been torn down or destroyed by fire. Two examples are the Mechanic's Institute, Lee's first wartime office, which stood on the west side of Ninth Street at Bank Street, and the Spotswood Hotel, where Lee lived when he came to Richmond in 1861; located at the southeast corner of Eighth and Main, it burned down the same year Lee died.

Perhaps the most famous no-longer-existing Lee site in Richmond once stood at the corner of Franklin and 14th Streets. Visitors who care to see it need travel only about four blocks south from the Museum of the Confederacy. The Ballard House and the Exchange Hotel once occupied the northeast and southeast corners of this intersection, and an elevated crosswalk ran between them.

Inside the Capitol is a statue marking the spot where Lee took command of Virginia's forces in 1861.

It was on March 26, 1870, just days before beginning his exhausting Southern tour, that Lee and his daughter Agnes were on the walkway between the two hotels when they ran into John Singleton Mosby. Once known as the "Gray Ghost," Mosby was a partisan ranger whom Lee had depended on to keep him informed of Federal movements in northern Virginia. Mosby was always a favorite of Lee's. Researchers have made the claim that his name appears as often in Lee's reports as that of any of his generals, though Mosby never rose above the rank of colonel. The two men agreed to meet for a chat in Lee's room. Mosby and Lee later enjoyed each other's company for a half-hour or more, though Mosby subsequently wrote that "the General looked pale and haggard, not like the Apollo I had known in the army."

Not long after leaving Lee's room, Mosby ran into another famous Confederate, former general George E. Pickett. Pickett expressed interest in seeing Lee again, but only if Mosby would accompany him. Mosby agreed. No mistake Mosby made in his war career likely matched that decision.

When Lee saw Pickett and Pickett saw Lee, an icy atmosphere settled over the room. Ever since July 3, 1863, when Pickett's Virginia division had been shattered while attacking Cemetery Ridge during the Pettigrew-Pickett-Trimble Assault at Gettysburg, relations between the two men had been declining. Pickett's reputation with Lee began to disintegrate when Pickett failed in a mission to free New Bern, North Carolina, in an aborted 1864 raid. Lee's support of Pickett collapsed entirely on April 2, 1865, when Pickett failed Lee's express order to hold Five Forks, Virginia, "at all costs." The loss of the cross-roads opened the way for the Federals to capture a nearby railroad line that cut off the last means of feeding Lee's army in Petersburg. When Five Forks fell, it essentially meant that Lee's army had to move out of Petersburg, or else it would starve. When Lee learned that Pickett had been eating lunch away from the battlefield when the Federals attacked at Five Forks, he mentally crossed Pickett off the list of officers upon whom he could depend. Not long before surrendering at Appomattox, Lee relieved Pickett of all command. When he saw him the next day still walking around camp, Lee asked derisively, "Is that man still with the army?"

Now, five years later, the two men faced each other for the last time. Lee, always known for forgiving the mistakes of poor-performing generals, never felt inclined that way toward Pickett. The two hardly looked at each other, a sign Mosby recognized as unrelenting animosity. After Mosby quickly ushered Pickett out of the room,

Lee called his home at 707 East Franklin "the Mess."

*The basement back door where Mathew Brady
took his famous photographs of Lee*

Pickett turned to Mosby and said, "That old man had my division
massacred at Gettysburg."

Perhaps the most significant building with a Lee connection still
standing in Richmond is the Capitol. Capitol Square is located about
three blocks south of the Museum of the Confederacy and west of the
site of Lee's confrontation with Pickett. The spot in the old House of
Delegates Chamber where Lee took command of Virginia's forces in
April 1861 has a statue of him. Virginia officials made his appointment
a flowery affair, which embarrassed Lee. Some of those same politicians later questioned his competence when he could not control the
actions of his subordinate generals in western Virginia. But at least
one future Confederate general recognized Lee's potential that day in
April. "We all felt at once that we had a leader worthy of the state and
the cause," wrote Jubal Early, a legislator from Lynchburg. Early later
served as one of Lee's most trusted subordinates. Lee lovingly dubbed
him "my mean old man" when Early became a division commander.

Lee did not have much love for politicians. Once, after returning

Lee worshiped at St. Paul's Episcopal Church when in Richmond.

from a visit to Richmond during which he begged legislators to find some way to find more food for his army, Lee bitterly remarked to an aide that all the politicians could do was "chew tobacco and eat peanuts."

Several blocks west on Franklin Street, at 707 East Franklin, is the home Lee called "the Mess," where Mrs. Lee lived during most of 1864 and where Lee returned in April 1865. According to witnesses, Lee had to walk through a crowd of admirers to enter the house upon his arrival after the war. He said nothing, acknowledging them with a dignified bow before entering the door for the last time as a soldier. The family lived here until moving in the summer of 1865 to Derwent, a house about 50 miles west of Richmond. Mrs. Lee and her daughters often held knitting parties in "the Mess," gathering to make socks for the soldiers.

It was less than a week after the general's return from Appomattox that Mathew Brady came knocking at the front door of this house asking for Lee to pose for a series of photographs. The photos were taken outside a basement back door that still exists, though it can't be

The Dabbs House was Lee's first headquarters.

seen from the street. The portraits of Lee alone and those with son Custis and aide Walter Taylor show an old, tired, but still very proud general who felt no shame for the fight over the last four years. They also marked the very first attempt at creating the legend of Robert E. Lee. The notion of Lee as icon was thus started by a Northerner, Brady. The back door's panels form a Christian cross. In each photo, Brady positioned Lee's head to emphasize the cross, tying the general forever to the image of a Christian soldier doing his duty. The placement of Lee and the cross in the door seem too perfect to have been a matter of chance.

The long-term fate of "the Mess" is still to be determined. The house was for sale at the time of this writing.

From Franklin and Eighth Streets, it is two blocks north and one block east to St. Paul's Episcopal Church, which stands on the corner of Ninth and Grace Streets. This is the Richmond church where Lee worshiped, sometimes with President Davis. The church is frequently open for visitors.

The last significant spot in urban Richmond associated with Lee is the Dabbs House, located on Nine Mile Road at the eastern edge of downtown near I-64. The building now houses the Henrico County Police Department's headquarters. As such, it is a public building, though it is not a museum. Historical markers in front describe its use by Lee.

The Dabbs House, once known as High Meadow, was Lee's first

Chickahominy Bluffs, where the Seven Days Campaign opened

headquarters. It was here that he met with his generals in June 1862 to plan for the Seven Days Campaign. Lee brought Thomas J. "Stonewall" Jackson, James Longstreet, A. P. Hill, D. H. Hill, and J. E. B. Stuart together for the first time as Confederate generals to discuss the defense of Richmond. It was at the Dabbs House that Lee and Stuart planned Stuart's famed "ride around McClellan," which resulted in Lee's discovery that the Union army's right flank was "in the air," meaning that it was not anchored to any natural defense. That virtually invited Lee to attack McClellan in order to draw the Federals away

Cold Harbor took place on virtually the same ground as the third day's fighting during the Seven Days.

Malvern Hill, where Lee made a tragic mistake in not calling off an infantry attack up the hill into the face of Union cannons.

from moving on Richmond. That attack at Beaver Dam Creek opened the Seven Days Campaign.

It was on Nine Mile Road not far from the Dabbs House that Jefferson Davis offered command to Lee.

Chickahominy Bluffs Battlefield Park lies east of the city, off Mechanicsville Turnpike near Laburnum Avenue. It was from these bluffs that Lee watched the opening of the Seven Days Campaign. This small unit of the National Park Service is open during daylight hours. It offers a few displays and some preserved earthworks Lee ordered constructed.

Beginning at Chickahominy Bluffs, interested visitors can follow the brown National Park Service signs tracing the action of the Seven Days in 1862 and Cold Harbor in 1864; Cold Harbor took place on virtually the same ground as the third day's fighting during the Seven Days. There are no marked sites specifically associated with Lee on National Park Service property. Lee spent most of the Seven Days riding up and down the roads, trying to figure out the poorly drawn maps and to coordinate his officers, who were all new to each other. The National Park Service tour ends at Malvern Hill, where Lee made a tragic mistake in not calling off an infantry attack up the hill into the face of Union cannons. Lee probably visited Malvern Hill as a child, as his grandfather's plantation, Shirley, is not far away.

Portsmouth/Norfolk

The Portsmouth waterfront is accessible at Water and High Streets near the Portsmouth Naval Shipyard Museum. The former home of Dr. William Selden is at the southwest corner of Freemason and Botecourt Streets in adjacent Norfolk. It is still a private home and is not open to the public.

On April 30, 1870, Lee entered Portsmouth by train, intending to quietly make the quick ferry ride across the Elizabeth River to meet his old chief of staff, Walter H. Taylor, in Norfolk. When Lee got off of the train, a crowd of former Confederate soldiers greeted him with the familiar Rebel yell. The embarrassed Lee boarded the ferry as the crowd pressed closer, hoping to experience his presence.

When Lee reached the Norfolk side of the river, Taylor met him among more Rebel yells, apparently taken up by old Norfolk soldiers who had heard their Portsmouth comrades. Lee was whisked by carriage to the home of Dr. William Selden, who had served as a surgeon in his army. The Selden House provided Lee a place to rest for several nights. On the Sunday morning after his arrival, his borrowed carriage had to carefully thread its way through respectful crowds so he could attend a nearby church. A couple of days later, Dr. Selden invited some hand-picked people for a small reception. Among the callers was Lee's former mess steward, the faithful Bryan, who had often carried out Lee's orders to redistribute any food sent to the general to men in the hospital.

Lee may have visited Taylor's house, located nearby at 227 West

Freemason. Taylor was only 23 when he joined Lee's staff. He served the general from the earliest days, though he sometimes sneaked away to take part in the fighting. He was so hurt by the surrender of the Army of Northern Virginia that he did not accompany Lee to the McLean House at Appomattox Court House. Several days later, however, Taylor was with Lee when they posed for a series of photographs taken by Mathew Brady at the back door of a house in Richmond.

Fort Monroe/Fort Wool

To visit Fort Monroe, take Exit 268 off I-64 in Hampton. Since this is an active military base, visitors must show photo identification. The Casemate Museum, located within the fort, is open daily. Admission is free. Call 757-727-3391 for information. Fort Wool, a small fort in Hampton Roads in front of Fort Monroe, is visible just northeast of the I-64 bridge before heading into the tunnel. The Hampton II *tour boat runs to Fort Wool from the Hampton Visitors Center between April and October; call 757-727-1102 for details.*

Work began on Fort Monroe, the only moat-surrounded fort still in active service of the United States Army, in 1819, but progress was slow. In May 1831, Lieutenant Lee arrived from his first posting at Fort Pulaski, Georgia, with orders to finish the outer works, a job that included supervising the construction of the moat. Lee was delighted to find that one of his old West Point friends, Lieutenant Joseph Johnston, was also assigned to the fort. Their paths would cross again 30 years later.

Lee arrived in 1831 with orders to finish the outer works for Fort Monroe.

The Casemate Museum is a fine facility that tracks the history of the fort right up to present times. Just outside the museum (and indicated by a historical marker) are the military quarters occupied for three years by Lieutenant Lee and his bride, Mary. Still military housing, the home was restored in recent years. It was in this house that the Lees' first child, George Washington Custis Lee, was born on September 16, 1832.

It was around that time, and perhaps at the fort, that Lee posed for his first portrait. The Benjamin West painting shows him in his

The Lees' first child was born in these military quarters in 1832.

black lieutenant's uniform with a high collar that seems to blend in with his rakish, long sideburns.

Lee left Fort Monroe in October 1834 for an assignment as assistant to the chief of engineers in Washington, D.C.

During his time in Hampton, Lee also worked on Fort Wool. His engineering skills were put to a considerable test there, as his duty was figuring where and how to place stones in order to build the foundation for a fort surrounded by water.

White Marsh

This mansion and the community of the same name are located off US 17 about seven miles north of Gloucester Point on the York River. The privately owned house is not visible from the highway.

Robert E. Lee stayed here only two nights, but what happened on the second evening is legendary in Virginia history.

In mid-May 1870, a very tired Lee was on the final stretch of his Southern tour when he was persuaded to visit White Marsh, the home of Dr. Prosser Tabb and his wife, Rebecca. Rebecca was a cousin of Lee's and one of the many women with whom he had corresponded through the years. Knowing that the aging general would be passing near her home on his way up from Norfolk heading toward Lexington, Mrs. Tabb persuaded him to stop so she could introduce him to her young family members, who knew Lee only by family and popular legend.

Lee and his son Robert Jr.—called "Rob" by the family—set out in a carriage for White Marsh from Rob's home, Romancoke in West

Lee spent two nights at White Marsh on the final stretch of his Southern tour in 1870.

Point, Virginia, about 20 miles away. In order to cross the York River, they loaded the carriage on a steamer. So many Virginians crowded the railing to see the old general that the captain had to order them to the other side in order to right the ship so Lee's carriage could unload on the north side of the York. By then, it was getting late in the day, and the temperature was dropping. Worried that his father would get chilled, Rob pushed his horse hard in order to get to White Marsh as quickly as possible. Once they arrived at the mansion, someone asked the 63-year-old Lee about the short trip. "I think Rob drives unnecessarily fast," the old man grumbled, demonstrating that the disenchantment of parents with their children's driving did not start with the invention of the automobile.

That evening, Lee and Rob slept in the same bed, which reminded the general of the times they used to do that when Rob was a toddler.

The next morning, Lee walked around the extensive gardens in front of and behind White Marsh and went for a carriage ride. His driver turned out to be one of his former soldiers, a man who had surrendered with Lee at Appomattox.

The man said, "I stuck with the army, but if you had in your entire command a greater coward than I was, you ought to have had him shot."

Lee was at once amused and touched, remembering how he had watched desertion deplete the army in the final days before the surrender. "That sort of coward makes a good soldier," he told Dr. Tabb.

That night, Lee turned down the family's request that he be the guest of honor at a community dinner. Instead, the Tabbs hosted a small family meal at which Lee was able to meet the young cousins, who looked at him with awe. After dinner, the family sat and talked in the parlor. The conversation turned to the heavy control of the South exerted by Reconstruction governments, which included occupation by Federal soldiers. Political and personal control over former Confederates was so strict that even old Confederate military buttons were banned from being worn on coats. One of the cousins asked the general what was to become of "us poor Virginians."

Lee's reply would filter out of the house that night and be printed in newspapers around Virginia. His attitude, as expressed in his answer, comforted and inspired Virginians long after his death. "You can work for Virginia, to build her up again, to make her great again. You can teach your children to love and cherish her," Lee said.

Those two simple sentences became the unofficial motto of Virginia during the 40 years it took the state to recover from the war and Reconstruction as it entered the 20th century.

The White House

This home is located in northern New Kent County on the west bank of the Pamunkey River, about three miles east of the community of Tunstall. From I-64, take Exit 214 on to VA 155 North. Follow this road across VA 249; the road becomes CR 608. After 5.7 miles, turn right on CR 614, a dirt road. In less than two miles, the road ends at White House Landing. About half a mile before the road ends, visitors will pass a gated dirt road on the right marked by No Trespassing signs mentioning the United States Navy. The house visible about a quarter-mile distant stands on White House Plantation.

White House Plantation, originally owned by the Custis family, was willed to Rooney, Lee's son, by his grandfather. The stone foundation of the White House is all that remains today; it lies to the west of the existing house.

The White House was doubly historic to Virginia, as it was the place where George Washington proposed to and may have married Martha Custis (records are unclear on the subject). Martha inherited the plantation upon the death of her first husband. The country was so proud of its first president that the White House in Washington was named after this White House. When Martha Washington died, the plantation came into the hands of George Washington Parke Custis, Mary Custis Lee's father.

Mary Lee stayed at the house after fleeing Arlington early in the war. When Union general George McClellan's troops came up the Pamumkey River during the Peninsula Campaign in May 1862, she fled only after tacking a note on the door. It read, "Northern soldiers who profess to revere Washington, forbear to desecrate the home of his first married life, the property of his wife, now owned by her descendants. A grand-daughter of Mrs. Washington." The note did no good. The Federals looted and burned the White House. Thousands of Union soldiers occupied the property around the landing.

After the war, both Rob and Rooney farmed the plantation. Lee visited the rebuilt house here.

Romancoke

This home is near the community of West Point, located on the York River at the junction of VA 33 and VA 30. Follow Main Street (VA 30) as it heads north from downtown West Point. Drive about two miles. Watch for West Point Christian Church on the left, then turn left on Euclid Street. Drive another two miles. Immediately after making a hard right turn, look to the left at the white house surrounded by a white fence at 2105 Euclid. The center part of this privately owned house (which is not open to the public) is Romancoke.

Romancoke was the home of Robert E. Lee, Jr. It sits on what was formerly one of the two Custis plantations willed to the Lee sons by their grandfather.

General Lee occasionally visited this house. In 1870, he was disappointed to find that his youngest son was not spending much time or money improving his home. Rob was a bachelor at the time and saw no need to have matching cups, saucers, and plates when there

Romancoke was the home of Robert E. Lee, Jr.

was no one around to appreciate them. The then-dilapidated house fit his needs. After making a few testy jokes about "the mansion" and the squalorous life of his son, the senior Lee let the matter drop. But he later bought Rob a matching set of silverware to use the next time he visited.

After his spring 1870 visit, the general never returned to the house. It was from here that Rob and the general left for their short jaunt to White Marsh.

This home was a favorite part-time residence of Rob's sisters, who often visited for months at a time after the general died.

The current owner of Romancoke says the two large trees in the backyard were planted by Rob.

Shirley Plantation

This plantation is located on VA 5 on the James River just south of Richmond. It is part of the James River Plantation Tour, which visits four plantations. It is open to visitors every day but Christmas; call 800-232-1613 or 804-829-5121 for details.

Lee's mother, Ann Hill Carter, was born at Shirley Plantation.

This house, completed in 1738 on land settled just six years after Jamestown, was the birthplace of Ann Hill Carter, the young woman who would marry former Revolutionary War general and former Virginia governor Henry "Light Horse Harry" Lee. The fourth of their children was Robert Edward Lee. Family history says Lee's mother caught a severe cold while returning from Shirley Plantation to her home at Stratford Hall because Harry had not sent a closed coach for her. She was very ill when Robert was born.

Robert E. Lee visited this house at least once a year while a child. Here, he developed a close relationship with his Carter cousins while his mother worried over what to do about her deteriorating marriage and the family's declining fortunes. Family history suggests that Lee may have attended classes in the converted laundry building during those visits.

Lee's son Rooney was married here in 1859. After the nearby Battle of Malvern Hill during the Seven Days Campaign of June 1862, the general made a brief stop to see if the property had been damaged by the Federal troops who had occupied plantations all along the James.

In 1868, Lee passed the house while riding a steamer on the James River. He wrote about standing on the deck hoping to see his cousins and wondering if he would ever lay eyes on his grandparents' house again. In May 1870, he got his wish when he spent two nights here before going to Romancoke and the White House to visit his sons.

A telling account of Lee's stature in the minds of Virginians—and even in the minds of his own family—was recorded by one of the Carter women, who observed the general quietly walking around the gardens outside the house during that brief visit. "We had heard of God, but here was General Lee!" she wrote.

Petersburg

I-85 and I-95 converge at Petersburg, which lies about 20 miles south of Richmond; travelers may also access the town via US 1 and US 460. Violet Bank is across the Appomattox River at the edge of the city of Colonial Heights, which borders Petersburg to the north. The Beasley House and St. Paul's Episcopal Church are two Lee sites in downtown Petersburg. The former site of Edge Hill and the Mayfield Bed-and-Breakfast lie to the west within the city. All of these attractions are within 10 minutes of Petersburg's visitor center.

During the time that Petersburg was under siege, Lee used several houses—or at least the property outside the houses—as headquarters. Lee was always reluctant to use private homes as headquarters, out of fear that the Federals would come along behind him and burn down the houses in retaliation against their civilian owners.

The best-preserved such home is Violet Bank, the yellow house on Virginia Avenue a block off Arlington Avenue at the edge of the neighboring town of Colonial Heights. Violet Bank is operated by

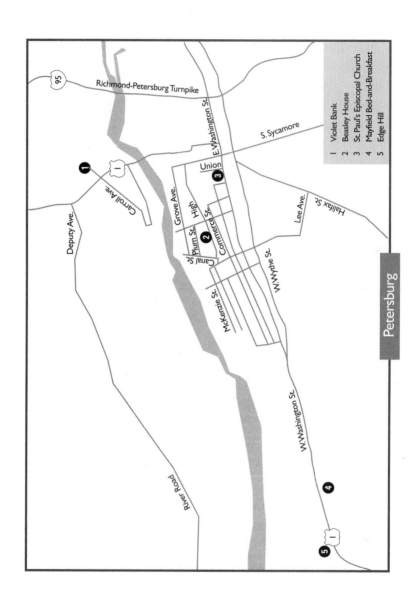

Map legend:
1 Violet Bank
2 Beasley House
3 St. Paul's Episcopal Church
4 Mayfield Bed-and-Breakfast
5 Edge Hill

Petersburg

95 — Richmond-Petersburg Turnpike

S. Sycamore
E. Washington St.
Union
Carroll Ave.
Deputy Ave.
Grove Ave.
High
Plum St.
Commerce St.
Canal St.
McKenzie St.
W. Wythe St.
Lee Ave.
Halifax St.
W. Washington St.
River Road

One of the best preserved houses that Lee used as his headquarters is Violet Bank.

Colonial Heights as a museum; it is open Tuesday through Sunday. The basement holds a number of interesting artifacts; the interior is a very well-preserved example of the Colonial style. Call 804-520-9395 for information.

Records seem to indicate that Lee pitched his tent in the front yard here in June 1864 and stayed until November. Legend says it was while camped under the giant cucumber tree (billed by the museum as the second-largest in the world) that Lee heard the explosion at the Crater on July 30, 1864. Lee was forced to abandon Violet Bank in November and move into Petersburg proper, as advancing Federals kept moving up their artillery. With the fall of the leaves on the high ground, Violet Bank made a tempting, exposed target.

Lee moved to the Beasley House at 558 High Street in downtown Petersburg for just over a month. This private house has a historical marker out front. Lee actually spent little time in or around the house. Instead, he kept riding along his lines, trying to keep Grant at bay. It was in this house, however, that Lee began to make written suggestions to President Davis that the Confederacy consider arming the South's slaves in hopes that they would add their manpower to the cause.

Also in the downtown area is St. Paul's Episcopal Church, located

Lee moved his headquarters to Beasley House in downtown Petersburg for just over a month.

on Union Street two blocks north of West Washington Street (US 1), less than a mile west of I-95. Lee worshiped in this church while in Petersburg. He returned to the church after the war to attend his son Rooney's wedding in November 1867. Much of the town turned out to see the general, who spent at least one night in the home of one of his old generals, William Mahone, who lived on the corner of Marshall and Sycamore Streets, several blocks south of the church.

In late November 1864, Lee moved from the Beasley House to Edge Hill, a home that stood two miles west near the intersection of Cox Road and Boydton Plank Road (US 1). This location served Lee better, since his lines were then extending farther west out of the city. Though irritated with his aides for moving into Edge Hill rather than staying in the yard, as had been his habit, Lee reluctantly gave in to the owner's insistence that he use it as his headquarters. Ironically, Lee's nicest accommodations during the whole war were also his last. He was at Edge Hill for four months. Once he left for the march toward Appomattox, he camped in a tent for the rest of the war.

It was at Edge Hill that Lee planned the attack on Fort Steadman. And he was here when he heard that Five Forks had fallen. It was also at Edge Hill that Lee experienced one of the dwindling moments of humor he was able to enjoy late in the war. One of the black soldiers serving in the army found his way to Lee's headquarters, apparently for no other purpose than to meet the general. Lee engaged the man in conversation and teased him that he did not appear to have been shot while serving in the Southern army. The man answered no, he had never been shot, because he made it a point to stay in the rear, where all the generals were. Lee retold the man's story many times to aides and visitors.

Edge Hill was shelled and burned just moments after Lee left it on April 2, 1865. A historical marker is near the site today.

One still-standing house with a tie to Lee is the Mayfield Bed-and-Breakfast at 3348 West Washington, not far from the site of Edge Hill. This house originally stood three-quarters of a mile farther west. Once Edge Hill came under Federal fire, Lee rode to Mayfield's original location and watched the fighting. It was likely at Mayfield that Lee got word that A. P. Hill had been killed by two Federal soldiers along Boydton Plank Road across from where the National Museum of the Civil War Soldier stands today.

ORANGE COURT HOUSE AREA

Culpeper

This town is located at the junction of US 15, US 522, and US 29 about midway between Fredericksburg and Harrisonburg. The Battle of Brandy Station was fought just a few miles north of Culpeper off what is now US 29; the Barbour House is the prominent brick home visible on the hill. The Battle of Cedar Mountain was fought just south of the town off what is now US 15.

The brick Barbour House is where Lee was staying when he found himself in the middle of the cavalry action during the Battle of Brandy Station.

Culpeper, Orange, and Gordonsville—three towns in a straight line on US 15 within 25 miles of each other—might be considered something like home base for the Army of Northern Virginia. Driving into the countryside from any of the towns will bring visitors to farmland that almost certainly served as campsites for the Confederate army. The Union army also camped around Culpeper.

After Lee's army recrossed the Potomac in September 1862 after the Battle of Sharpsburg, the soldiers moved to the vast fields surrounding Culpeper, thinking they would set up here for winter encampments. The general likely dined on occasion at the boyhood home of A. P. Hill, on the northwest corner of Main and Davis Streets. Lee was in a headquarters tent set up in an unnamed pine thicket at Culpeper in October when he got word that his daughter Annie had died of fever at a springs in North Carolina. Circumstances did not permit him to go to her funeral. Responding to the threat of Burnside's move on Fredericksburg, Lee and his army rushed to the southeast in early December.

The Battle of Brandy Station was fought on June 9, 1863. Lee found himself in the middle of the cavalry action while staying at the Barbour House. The Federal cavalry surprised and attacked

J. E. B. Stuart's cavalry on this battlefield, only a day after Stuart had shown off his cavalry to his commander, Lee, in a grand review. A mightily embarrassed Stuart would have been even more chagrined if his boss had been captured at the Barbour House. The Federals swept up the hill several times but never got close to Lee. They apparently never knew the commander of the Army of Northern Virginia was close by. The site where Lee watched the grand review is now a Virginia Highway Patrol headquarters about two miles south of Brandy Station on CR 762, a secondary highway paralleling US 29 to the east.

Orange Court House

The town of Orange is about 15 miles south of Culpeper on US 15; VA 20 also runs through the village. St. Thomas Episcopal Church is at 119 Caroline Street in the downtown area. The site of Lee's field headquarters is off VA 20 less than two miles east of downtown.

After Lee retreated from Gettysburg in the summer of 1863, he established headquarters in Orange Court House. He spent the winter of 1863 through the spring of 1864 here, then left to start the Wilderness Campaign.

Lee attended St. Thomas Episcopal Church during the months he was here. The pew where he sat is marked.

It was at his field headquarters tent east of Orange Court House that Lee tried to resign command of the Army of Northern Virginia. In a letter to President Jefferson Davis about two weeks after the loss at Gettysburg, he wrote that he knew the press was critical of his decisions. He also stated that, though he had heard no criticism from his officers or men, he supposed it existed. "I therefore, in all sincerity, request Your Excellency to take measures to supply my place," Lee wrote. Later, he explained, "Everything points to the advantages to be derived from a new commander, and I the more anxiously urge the matter upon Your Excellency from my belief that a younger and abler man than myself can readily be obtained."

Davis answered within a few days: "Where will I find that new commander who is to posses the greater ability which you believe to be required?" He later added, "To ask me to substitute you by some one in my judgement more fit to command, or who would possess more of the confidence of the army, or of the reflecting men of the country, is to demand an impossibility."

Lee let the matter drop. He did not try to resign again.

It was also at this field headquarters that Lee lost his wartime pet, a chicken. Lee had kept the chicken for nearly two years, as it produced an egg nearly every day. One day, Lee's cook, without the general's knowledge, killed the chicken and served it for dinner when Lee was entertaining an important guest.

A historical marker stands at the site of the headquarters today.

Clark's Mountain was maintained as a
Confederate observation post throughout the war.

Clark's Mountain

This mountain may be accessed from VA 20 about five miles east of downtown Orange; watch to the north for the radio towers that mark Clark's Mountain. Turn north on to CR 628 (Clifton Road). Drive three and a half miles, then turn right on CR 627 (Clark Mountain Road). Drive one mile, then turn left on CR 697. This county roads ends on private property on top of Clark's Mountain; please do not trespass. Stay on the road to get the same commanding view of the land north and east of Orange that Lee got. Using binoculars, you should be able to see the Rappahannock River in the distance.

The most important spot to Lee in this region was Clark's Mountain, maintained as a Confederate observation post throughout the war. It was while studying two different Union armies—the Army of Virginia under General John Pope and later the Army of the Potomac under Generals U. S. Grant and George Meade—from Clark's Mountain that Lee developed the strategy for Second Manassas in 1862 and the Wilderness Campaign in 1864.

In 1862, Lee could see through Confederate telescopes set up on this spot that Pope was putting his army between the Rappahannock and the Rapidan Rivers on the north and south. Lee reasoned if he could cut Pope off on the east by sending in his cavalry, he could sweep in from the west and virtually destroy the army. But before Lee could advance his army to catch the enemy in this natural bottleneck, Pope recognized his mistake and extracted his army. In response to this lost opportunity, Lee sent Jackson rushing toward Pope's rear at Manassas, which resulted in the Battle of Second Manassas.

In 1864, Lee watched again as Grant pushed across Germana Ford on the Rapidan and into the Wilderness. Lee believed the region was so tangled with undergrowth that Grant would not be able to maneuver. He rushed his army forward to catch the Federals in the woods.

Gordonsville

This town lies about 10 miles south of Orange at the junction of US 15 and US 33.

Lee was in and out of Gordonsville frequently because it was the location of two vital railroads, the Orange & Alexandria (which ran through Orange and Culpeper) and the Virginia Central (which ran to the east near Richmond). On occasion, he worshiped with Stonewall Jackson in the Presbyterian church on VA 33 about a quarter-mile south of the traffic circle. He boarded the train at the Exchange Hotel, a half-mile

On occasion, Lee worshiped with Stonewall Jackson at this Presbyterian Church in Gordonsville.

south of the circle. The old hotel, which served as a Confederate hospital during the war, is now a museum that specializes in interpreting Civil War medicine; call 540-832-2944 for information.

Derwent

This home is in Powhatan County, just west of Richmond. From US 60 near the town of Powhatan, turn north on CR 629 (Trenholm Road). Drive about two and a half miles, then turn left on Derwent Road. The home is at the end of the road, but please admire it only from the photo in this book, as the access drive and the home itself are private. The site of Lee's last night in the field is about 10 miles from Derwent, on VA 711 about four and a half miles east of the intersection with VA 522. The campsite is now at the entrance to a housing development.

When the war ended, all General Lee wanted to do was retire someplace where he could try to forget the horrible sights he had experienced. He did not want any of his old officers—or historians, reporters, or admirers—coming to see him. He considered himself retired. All he wanted to do was find himself a country home where he could live out his last years in peace.

Offers came from around the state and even from out of the country. One Englishman offered him the use of a country estate in Great Britain, but Lee wrote back, "I cannot desert my native state in the hour of her adversity."

Lee's options were also limited due to some talk of charging him with treason against the United States for his role in leading the Army of Northern Virginia. For a while, it appeared that the charge would escalate from an indictment to a full arrest and trial, but Lee's old foe, General U. S. Grant, made it clear that he would not stand by while the United States violated the parole and surrender agreement he had signed with Lee. Grant threatened to resign from the army if Lee was arrested. Eventually, the government backed down on arresting Lee, though it did arrest Jefferson Davis and imprison him in Fort Monroe, Lee's old post.

In the summer of 1865, Mrs. Elizabeth Cocke wrote Lee—then living in a rented home on Franklin Street in Richmond—a letter offering him a house in Powhatan County near the James River. Probably without even seeing it, Lee agreed. In July, he packed up the meager family goods and moved with Mrs. Lee, son Custis, and daughters Mary and Mildred to the farmhouse called Derwent about 55 miles west of Richmond.

Mrs. Cocke likely furnished the house simply, as the Lees may have brought some furniture with them from Richmond. It was a relatively simple two-over-two farmhouse (meaning that each floor, including the basement, had just two rooms). It was nothing like Arlington, where Mrs. Lee had grown up, or the busy house on Franklin Street in Richmond, where Lee had returned after Appomattox. For

During the summer of 1865, the Lee family lived at Derwent until Lee accepted the presidency of Washington College in Lexington.

nearly four months, Derwent was Lee's sanctuary away from the city. Here, he could write letters, visit with his family, and contemplate his future.

It was in August that a total stranger came to see Lee at Derwent with startling news—he had been nominated for the presidency of Washington College in Lexington. Lee knew about the school, since one of his stepbrothers had attended there, but he had never so much as visited. He had not applied for the president's job, but the school's board of trustees, shrewdly thinking of someone who would bring in more students, had nominated him.

In response to the offer, Lee wrote one of his typical letters that is hard for modern readers to understand. In the letter, he told the trustees that he would not take the job because his name would be a lightning rod of controversy. He then told them that if they didn't believe he would cause the school trouble, he would take the job. He ended by saying he would decline the job unless the trustees thought he was the man to take it. In the course of one letter, Lee seemingly rejected the offer three times and accepted it twice. Once the board received Lee's letter, it affirmed that Lee was the proper man and issued a public statement that he would be the new president.

Lee left Derwent on September 15, 1865, heading for Lexington, more than 100 miles away. He rode alone on Traveller, stopping at friends' houses along the way. The family followed in early December by taking a river barge. No members of the family ever visited Derwent again.

Today, Derwent looks better than it did when the Lees occupied it. At some point after their stay, it was virtually abandoned. A local historian subsequently rescued it and restored it to its 1865 appearance. Two wings were added in 1983 in order to make it a livable home by modern standards; the wings were designed to look as if they were part of the original house. The central portion of Derwent still appears the same as it did the summer Lee spent in it.

General and Mrs. Lee presumably lived on the first floor, as Mrs. Lee was in a wheelchair and was unable to climb stairs. The two daughters and Custis used the upstairs bedrooms. Custis actually lived at the home of Derwent's owner for several weeks, due to an illness he acquired on the trip into the country.

It was by coincidence that Derwent was situated near the route that Lee took from Appomattox to Richmond. Lee's last night in the field (two nights after leaving the surrender) was spent right across the road from his brother Charles Lee's farmhouse, located about 10 miles east of Derwent. Charles Lee's house is out of sight down a private road on the opposite side of VA 711. A historical marker is located on the road.

Amelia Court House

This little town sits on US 360 Business at the intersection with VA 38 about 30 miles west of Richmond and about 30 miles east of Appomattox. The railroad siding where Lee's heart was broken is on the north side of the village. Church Street is in the town's southern section.

When Lee and his army reached the railroad siding at Amelia Court House on April 4, 1865, he was expecting to find at least 350,000 rations of meat and bread, an emergency reserve that had been stored in Richmond. Lee had telegrammed the government on April 2 that he would be heading toward Amelia Court House and that he would need to feed his men if they were to continue in the field.

For reasons historians still have not sorted out, the food was never loaded on the train cars. The telegram was somehow lost in the confusion of the evacuation of the city and the fleeing of the Confederate Cabinet. The only thing in the cars was ammunition.

One officer wrote of watching Lee when he looked inside the cars: "I shall never forget the broken-hearted expression his face wore or the still sadder tones of his voice. No one who looked upon him then, as he stood there in full view of the disastrous end, can ever forget the intense agony written upon his features. And yet he was calm, self-possessed and deliberate."

It was somewhere on Church Street in Amelia Court House that Lee saved a Union soldier from certain death. A Federal patrol had stumbled on to the Confederates, and one of their cavalrymen was riding toward the Confederate lines. The Confederates were about to fire on the man when Lee himself shouted, "Don't shoot!" When the cavalryman continued riding into Confederate lines, what Lee had seen was confirmed—the man was so badly wounded that he couldn't control his horse.

Sayler's Creek

This battlefield is located at the junction of CR 617 (St. James Road) and CR 618; the site is north of US 360 between Amelia Court House and Farmville. A monument stands at the top of a hill off CR 617 on the south side of Sayler's Creek.

Sayler's Creek is the site of Lee's last, depressing battle, which told him that the time had come to end the fighting. Sayler's Creek Battlefield is now a Virginia State Battlefield. It was on this rolling ground that the Army of Northern Virginia found itself cut into four parts by

Sayler's Creek is the site of Lee's last battle.

Site where Lee watched the Battle of Sayler's Creek

the overwhelming strength of the pursuing Federals. More than 8,000 Confederates and eight Confederate generals were captured here on April 6, 1865.

CR 617 passes the Hillsman Farmhouse, a preserved home used as a hospital by the Federals. It was from the hill across the creek that Lee observed his army being sliced apart. Watching hungry, depressed, frightened soldiers and officers streaming past him, Lee cried out, "My God! Has the army been dissolved?" That night, he wrote a message to President Davis that the army could not stand many more battles like the one here.

Farmville

This town is located at the junction of US 460 and VA 45 about 20 miles east of Appomattox. Cumberland Church is on VA 45 about three miles north of town.

A stone historical marker in downtown Farmville notes the former site of a hotel that boasted a unique distinction at the end of the war:

A stone historic marker notes the former site of a hotel in Farmville where Lee spent one night and Grant spent the next.

Lee spent one night there and Grant the next. Just north of downtown is a sign in a parking lot next to a railroad crossing showing where Lee's army finally received some food supplies.

It was at an unidentified cottage near Cumberland Church on the evening of April 7, 1865, that Lee received his first note from U. S. Grant asking for the surrender of the Army of Northern Virginia. The Federal officer who delivered it to one of Lee's pickets was Brigadier

In an unidentified cottage near Cumberland Church, Lee received his first note from Grant asking for his surrender.

General Seth Williams, who had been adjutant (chief assistant) to Lee during Lee's tenure as superintendent at West Point. Williams carried several notes back and forth between Grant and Lee over the next two days, but it is doubtful that Lee ever saw him until the day of surrender.

Lee looked at that first note from Grant and handed it to Longstreet without comment. Longstreet read the note and then said, "Not yet." Lee scrawled a reply to Grant asking the conditions under which he would accept a surrender.

Clifton

This home is just west of the intersection of CR 636 and US 15 northwest of Farmville and about four miles east of the community of New Store.

Clifton is the two-story house where Grant was spending the night when he finally received a note from Lee suggesting that a surrender was possible.

It was in nearby New Store that Lee did something that seems strange—he took the time to formally relieve command of George Pickett, Bushrod Johnson, and Richard H. Anderson. In other words, at a time when he needed every man, he ordered three generals out of the army. It was a rare display of misplaced anger by Lee, who still simmered over the Battle of Sayler's Creek, where the three generals had lost most of their commands.

Appomattox Court House

Appomattox Court House is on VA 24 about 20 miles east of Lynchburg. New Hope Church is on VA 24 about two miles northeast of the National Historical Park.

It was at New Hope Church on April 8, 1865, that Lee himself went out under a white flag and personally carried a note offering to meet with Grant. After an exchange of notes, the Federals on his front politely told Lee that Grant was not anywhere nearby where he could receive the note. They then thoughtfully informed him that they intended to attack that front and that it would be wise for him to move out of their range. Twice before—at the Wilderness and Spotsylvania Court House—Confederates had ordered, "Lee to the rear!" Now, admiring Federal soldiers were giving him the same order.

The site of Lee's last battlefield headquarters lies about two miles southwest of New Hope Church off VA 24, at the outskirts of the village of Appomattox Court House. Visitors may leave their vehicles in the National Park Service parking lot and walk to the top of the hill to experience the site.

It was in these woods that Lee made the last of his war decisions. It was here that he met with his generals—Longstreet, John Gordon, and nephew Fitz Lee—for the last time, in order to discuss whether there was any way they could fight their way through the Federals now in their front.

It was here that Lee made his last wartime joke. When one of Gordon's aides asked Lee how far he would suggest Gordon march his troops, Lee answered, "Tell General Gordon I should be glad for him to halt just beyond the Tennessee line," nearly 200 miles distant.

It was here that Lee donned a brand-new dress uniform and

The site of Lee's last battlefield headquarters lies at the outskirts of the village of Appomattox Court House.

strapped on a fancy sword, reasoning that if he were to be made a prisoner of war by the end of the day, he should look his best.

It was here the day after the surrender that Lee entertained an old army friend, General George Meade, the nominal commander of the Union's Army of the Potomac. Lee joked that Meade had more gray in his beard than the last time they had spoken. Meade answered, "You are to blame for that." Later that same day, Lee received another visitor from the Union army, General Henry Hunt, the master of artillery who had outdueled the Confederate guns on battlefields like Malvern Hill and Gettysburg. It was a mark of the discipline still left in the Confederate army that two Union generals could visit Lee in complete safety two days before the Confederates would turn in their weapons.

It was here on this hill on April 10, 1865, that Lee wrote out his last order, General Order Number 9, which formally told his troops that they were surrendered but that they should "take with you the satisfaction that proceeds from the consciousness of duty faithfully performed."

Lee stayed camped in these woods from April 8 through April 12. He did not attend the final stacking of arms, which took place on the courthouse lawn.

Farther southwest on VA 24, there is a historical marker on the left where the road descends toward a creek. This was the site where Lee rested in an orchard just before riding into Appomattox. It was here that he received his last visit from Longstreet not long before he went to meet with Grant. The Old Warhorse, who often counseled Lee against waging offensive battles, particularly at Gettysburg, now told Lee that unless Grant offered "honorable terms," they should continue fighting. Lee did not answer. He had already made up his mind that the fighting would end. Lee and Longstreet would never see each other again, but they wrote lengthy, friendly letters to each other. Lee would never join the faction of his generals who accused Longstreet of losing Gettysburg by his reluctance to fight in the open.

It was also in this orchard that Lee exhibited one of his last displays of anger. After the surrender, he had returned to the orchard to await some of the documents that would formalize the process. He was pacing up and down, unable to relax now that his part of the war was over. Several Union officers arrived and asked to be presented to him. They wanted to see the man who had galvanized the South for the last three years. Lee glared at them. He did not want to be put on display for his enemies.

Visitors who look southwest while crossing the creek can see the grass roadbed that is the route Lee took while riding to and from the surrender. On April 9, it was lined with crying Confederates who reached out to Lee as he passed. Some of them told him they were still willing to fight for him.

There are three significant Lee sites in the restored Appomattox village.

Just north of the visitor center is a historical marker that describes a meeting between Lee and Grant on the day after the surrender. Grant asked Lee if he would write a letter urging all of the other Confederate armies in the field to surrender. Lee politely declined, pointing out that he was only a general, not the commander in chief. He had no authority to suggest that other generals surrender their

Site where Lee met Grant for the last time at Appomattox

armies. Grant acknowledged that Lee was correct and went on his way. The two would meet again briefly several years later in the White House, when Grant was president.

The second site is a field lying several hundred yards west. Lee rode here early on the morning of April 9 to see if it was possible for his men to cut their way through the Federals blocking the road. He sent word to General Gordon asking what was happening in front of him. Gordon replied that his corps "was fought to a frazzle." After hearing this report, Lee said to his staff officers, "There is nothing left for me to do but to go and see General Grant, and I would rather die a thousand deaths." It was also here that Lee absently contemplated suicide, saying, "How easily I could be rid of this, and be at rest! I have only to ride along the line and all will be over!"

Lee had some second thoughts about surrendering while pacing this field. Twice, he asked Longstreet if surrender was the right decision, and twice Longstreet agreed. At Lee's request, General Porter Alexander answered a question about what the army should do. Alexander suggested that it scatter into the mountains without formally surrendering or agreeing to end the war. That way, some of the men could reach Joe Johnston's army in North Carolina. Lee listened but then rejected the idea, saying that the men were already demoralized and that they would have to resort to bushwhacking. He told

The reconstructed McLean House, an exact duplicate of the original, which was dismantled after the war

Alexander the whole army would surrender. Lee's decision saved countless lives and ended a war that could have dragged on for years.

The third site is the reconstructed McLean House, an exact duplicate of the original, which was dismantled after the war. Lee met Grant in the front parlor. It was here that Lee finally met General Seth Williams, who had acted as a courier between the Union and Confederate forces. Lee was polite to his old acquaintance but was in no mood to talk over old times. When Lee spied Colonel Ely Parker, an Iroquois Indian, he smiled slightly and made a comment about how it was nice to see "a real American" in the room. It was here that Lee asked Grant for 25,000 rations for his men.

After about a half-hour, Lee left the McLean House. As Lee was riding Traveller through the yard, a *New York Tribune* reporter turned to Confederate general Armistead Long. The reporter pointed to Lee and asked, "Who is that distinguished-looking officer?"

An incredulous Long stared long and hard at the ignorant reporter before answering, "That is the greatest man the county ever produced, General Robert E. Lee."

Warm Springs/Hot Springs

Warm Springs is about 41 miles northwest of Lexington on VA 39. Hot Springs is a few miles south of Warm Springs on US 220.

The two bathhouses at Warm Springs—one for men and one for women—are still open, though they are not the originals that Lee and his wife used. The current bathhouses were built after the war but likely look very similar to those of earlier days. Lee never seemed to believe in the healing powers of springs, but he loved his wife enough to take her to these health spas of their day and keep her company.

Lee also visited nearby Hot Springs, now the site of the Homestead Resort. Hot Springs was the last vacation spot at which he spent a week, starting August 9, 1870. From his letters, it appears that Lee understood his life was winding down; he was experiencing physical pain and feelings of unease with his health. His stay at the resort helped; in fact, he made mention of it in the last letter he wrote, in early September 1870. Today's Homestead is not the original building. The modern incarnation is a golf resort different in character from the healing springs of years gone by.

Mrs. Lee would spend time at this cottage when the general went to Warm Springs or Hot Springs.

Rockbridge Baths

These baths are about 11 miles northwest of downtown Lexington on VA 39.

In its day, Rockbridge Baths was a small resort where one could take "healing" baths. The little yellow cottage on the south side of the road just before the village is where Mrs. Lee used to spend time. A famous photograph of Lee wearing a straw hat and sitting on Traveller was taken behind this cottage. Particularly good prints of this photo show a line of mountains to match the actual peaks visible beyond the cottage's backyard. The cottage is a private home today, so please do not trespass.

Lexington

The town is situated at the very upper (southern) end of the Shenandoah Valley off I-81. US 60 runs through Lexington, and the Blue Ridge Parkway is just to the east.

It was in Lexington that Lee found peace after four years of war. He lived, vacationed, and worked in this area for five years, the longest time he spent in one place his entire adult life.

Lexington is the home of Washington and Lee University, called Washington College when Lee was asked to become its president in the fall of 1865. Though he had tried to beg off heading the United States Military Academy in the 1850s, Lee did not hesitate to take the job of president of this small, struggling school.

Visitors will certainly want to see the Lee House, the college president's house that Lee virtually designed for himself and his wheel-chair-bound wife. It is located three blocks west of Main Street right off Washington Street. The home's porch wraps all the way around

These buildings at Washington and Lee University look much as they did when Lee assumed the presidency of the college in the fall of 1865.

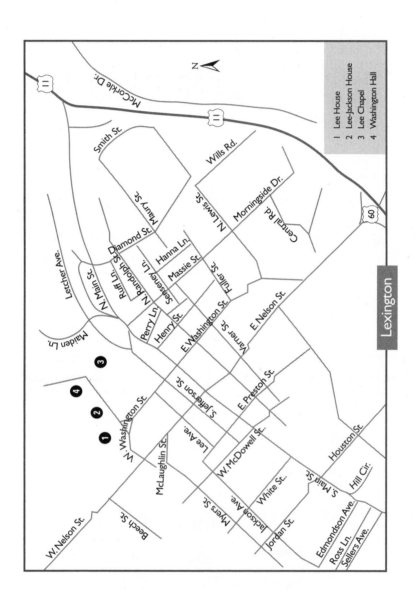

Lexington

1 Lee House
2 Lee-Jackson House
3 Lee Chapel
4 Washington Hall

The Lee House, where Lee and his family lived while he served as president of the college.

the structure, so Mrs. Lee could get around it easily. The garage was once the stable for Traveller and another favorite Lee horse, Lucy Long. Lee designed the stable to be attached to the house, as he wanted to be able to say that Traveller, in his retired years, was living under his owner's roof. The house is still occupied by the Washington and Lee president and is not open to the public, though the garage is traditionally left open so visitors can see where Traveller lived.

It was to this house that Lee came on September 28, 1870, after attending a meeting of a church building committee. At dinner, his wife and daughters noticed that he was in distress, unable to speak. When the doctor arrived, the old general made a few comments. A bed was brought down from the upstairs and set up in the bay window that can be seen on the north side of the house. From there, the general could see the mountains in the distance. He lay in his bed from September 28 until the morning of October 12, when he slipped away. The cause of death likely was a combination of pneumonia, heart problems he had known about for 17 years, and perhaps a slight stroke.

Beside the Lee House is a structure that may be even more historically significant. It is the Lee-Jackson House. The north wing of this home was first occupied in 1853 by Professor Thomas J. Jackson, who had married the college president's daughter. In 1865, Lee and

The Lee-Jackson House was first occupied by Professor Thomas J. Jackson in 1853. Lee and his family lived here while the Lee House was being constructed.

his family lived here while the Lee House was being constructed.

Behind the houses is Washington Hall, the primary building of the university when Lee was president. The room where he took his oath of office as president is on the second floor; it is marked by a plaque.

In front of Washington Hall is what most tourists come to see in Lexington: Lee Chapel. Though Lee was a devout Episcopalian, he had the foresight to make the chapel nondenominational. He was also practical. The chapel was never officially made a church, so the school often used it as a lecture hall. Designed by Lee's son Custis, the chapel was started when Washington College had only 40 students. It is designed to accommodate 600. The chapel is open daily except for Thanksgiving, Christmas, and New Year's; call 540-463-8768 for information.

The statue at the front of the chapel does not depict Lee in death, as many tourists assume, but rather sleeping on his cot, as he did on the battlefield. It was modeled from life not long before Lee began his final illness.

Below the statue in the basement of the building is the Lee crypt, which contains the general's remains, as well as those of his immediate family.

Lee Chapel was designed by Lee's son Custis. The Lee crypt, which contains the general's remains and those of his immediate family, is in the basement of the building.

Beyond the crypt is a fine museum to Lee's life. It has some very interesting exhibits, including sketches Lee made of snapping turtles and alligators when he was stationed at Fort Pulaski, Georgia, and a model of the famous feathered shako hat still worn by the cadets at West Point.

Outside the museum is Lee's office, said to be exactly as he left it on the day he became ill. Correspondence and books lie scattered around the table, looking as if he intended to return to his work the next morning. The last thing Lee did as president of the college was autograph a photograph of himself for a student who was waiting outside his office door.

Right outside the door to the office is Traveller's grave. Traveller liked to graze the campus. While doing so one day, he picked up a rusty nail in his hoof. It became infected, and he died just seven months

Right outside the door of Lee's office is Traveller's grave. Visitors often leave apples and other souvenirs on this gravesite.

after the general. Right up until the general's last illness, man and horse were a familiar sight riding through the mountains around Lexington.

Natural Bridge/Peaks of Otter

The Natural Bridge is about 15 miles south of Lexington just off I-81 at Exit 175. The sharp-tipped mountain known as the Peaks of Otter is located on the Blue Ridge Parkway about 25 miles south of Lexington.

South of Lexington are two other tourist spots that Lee enjoyed.

Coming back from a trip to the Peaks of Otter in 1869, Lee and his daughter Mildred stopped to marvel at the Natural Bridge, a large stone arch. Ironically, this natural formation was once owned by Thomas Jefferson, a political enemy of Lee's father, Light Horse Harry Lee.

Earlier, Lee and Mildred, one of his more adventurous daughters, had climbed to the top of the Peaks of Otter after riding their horses most of the way up the path. Lee sat down and gazed out at the valley below him without saying a word.

That afternoon, they were riding east hoping to spend the night in a distant town when a thunderstorm caught them. Lee and his daughter barged into a mountain cabin to get away from the storm. The woman of the house, irritated at the strangers tracking mud and water on her clean floors, did not recognize the old general, though her husband had a portrait of Lee hanging on the wall. It wasn't until Lee's daughter told the woman who he was that she recognized the most recognizable man in the South.

A walking path still leads to the top of the Peaks of Otter today. At its base is a motel managed for the National Park Service.

Executive Office Building/
Blair House/White House

The three Lee sites in the city may all be viewed from Pennsylvania Avenue. Only the White House offers regular public tours.

Robert E. Lee, the Confederacy's most famous general, is not often associated with the seat of Federal power. But it was discussions in Washington that helped make Lee the icon he is today.

The circumstances surrounding Lee's visits to Washington remain historically murky, and the timing of events seems curious.

The newly elected Abraham Lincoln, sworn in as president on March 4, 1861, apparently recognized early in his administration (or maybe even before taking office) that the existing head of the army, 75-year-old Winfield Scott, no longer had the vigor to manage the military matters of the United States. At the same time, Lincoln must have understood that few people other than General Scott knew men who could lead the Union to victory. Records do not indicate any meetings between the two before Lincoln's inauguration, but Lincoln

Lee met with Winfield Scott in what is now the Executive Office Building in March 1861 to discuss his future.

and Scott or their aides must have met or corresponded to discuss who the general believed should head the army in the event of his retirement.

Around that same time, Scott was thinking about a soldier he had known from the Mexican War in 1847, Robert E. Lee. In February 1861, General Scott ordered Lieutenant Colonel Lee back from his posting in Texas to Washington. Lee arrived home in Arlington on March 1, just three days before Lincoln's inauguration. He immediately went to meet with Scott in his office in the State, War, and Navy Building (what is now the vice president's office in the Executive Office Building, located next to the White House). Neither Lee nor Scott recorded what was said during the three-hour meeting, but Scott was described as "painfully quiet" after Lee left. It has been speculated that he may have offered Lee a command at the meeting, which he was certainly not authorized to do. If he did, Lee likely replied much as he had to friends in Texas: if Virginia left the Union, he would have no choice but to leave with it. About the only thing known for certain to have come out of the meeting was that Lee was promoted from lieutenant colonel to full colonel.

There seems to have been little communication between Lee and his superiors over the next six weeks, as everyone in the country watched the political situation unfold. During that time, about two weeks after the meeting with Scott, Lee received an offer of a generalship from the new Confederacy. He ignored the letter. He was a Virginian and an officer in the United States Army, not a Confederate. While Lee was home, Virginia twice voted not to secede from the Union.

Things changed on April 12, 1861, when South Carolina fired on Fort Sumter. On April 15, Lincoln called for 75,000 volunteers to invade the South and ordered Virginia to supply several regiments.

On April 17, the same day Virginia voted to secede in response to Lincoln's call for troops, Lee received two notes. One was from Scott, asking to meet in his office a second time. The other was from Francis P. Blair, Sr., a man Lee had never met but who was the father of Montgomery Blair, a friend from his engineering days in St. Louis.

A curious Lee rode into Washington to Blair House on April 18 (located opposite the White House and today used by the government as an official guest house for visiting foreign dignitaries). There, Blair apparently offered Lee what Scott may have offered a month earlier: field command of the Federal army. Blair made it clear that the offer came with the full blessing of both Secretary of War Simon Cameron and President Lincoln. Lee immediately rejected the offer, saying he would "return to my native state and share the miseries of my people." He further told Blair that "though opposed to secession and deprecating war, I could take no part in an invasion of the Southern states."

From Blair House, Lee walked across Pennsylvania Avenue to Scott's office. Judging by Scott's expectant reception of Lee, the old general must have known about the meeting with Blair. Scott may have asked Blair to set up the meeting so Lee would know that the offer came from President Lincoln himself, and not just from Scott. When Lee told Scott what he had said to Blair, Scott replied, "Lee, you have just made the greatest mistake of your life, but I feared it would be so." Scott ended the meeting with an admonition to Lee that he should resign immediately.

Lee's only visit to the White House was in late spring when he met for 15 minutes with President U.S. Grant.

On April 19, Lee learned that his state had seceded. On April 20, he resigned from the United States Army. On April 21, he received orders to report to Richmond to take command of Virginia's forces. On April 22, he left Arlington.

The only time Lee was in the White House was in the late spring of 1869, when he met for just 15 minutes with President U. S. Grant while passing through on his way from Baltimore to Alexandria. Little was recorded about the meeting, other than that the two old foes exchanged pleasantries and seemed saddened by their talk.

Harpers Ferry

The town is about 10 miles south of Shepherdstown via WV 230. The visitor center for Harpers Ferry National Historic Park is on US 340 about two miles from the historic district. The park is open every day except Christmas; call 304-535-6298 for information.

It was at Harpers Ferry that Robert E. Lee first became a nationally known figure to the press and the public.

Lee was at home in Arlington on October 17, 1859, when Lieutenant J. E. B. Stuart knocked on his door with an urgent message from the War Department asking that he come to the office immediately. When Lee arrived, he learned that some sort of slave insurrection was occurring in Harpers Ferry. Lee and Stuart rushed by train to the town; Lee didn't even bother putting on his officer's uniform, arriving in civilian clothes.

In Harpers Ferry, Lee learned that he, a lieutenant colonel in the United States Army, would have to command a company of United States Marines and a company of Virginia militia, units he would never have had contact with under normal circumstances.

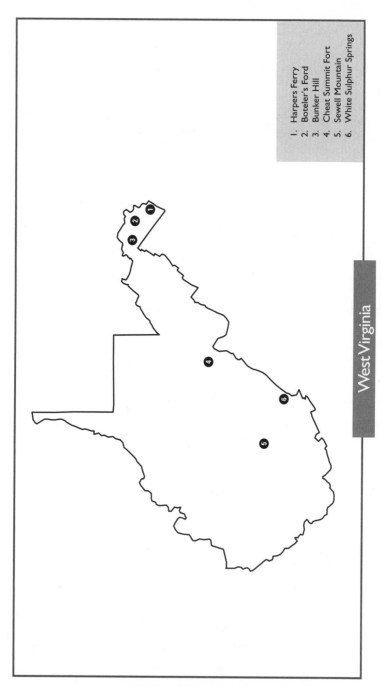

West Virginia

1. Harpers Ferry
2. Boteler's Ford
3. Bunker Hill
4. Cheat Summit Fort
5. Sewell Mountain
6. White Sulphur Springs

IN THE FOOTSTEPS OF ROBERT E. LEE

The Engine House, where John Brown and his co-conspirators were surrounded by Lee and his forces.

He established headquarters in the Armorer's House, then took complete control of the situation. First, he determined that the threat was contained, since all of the armed conspirators were holed up in the Engine House, which was surrounded. He then telegraphed Fort Monroe that more troops would not be needed. He kept folded an order giving him the power to declare martial law in the city. Lee began to form a plan to storm the Engine House.

Around midnight, he got word that John Brown, a well-known abolitionist who had hacked a slave-owning family to death in Kansas several years earlier, might be the leader of the mixed band of white and black insurgents. On the morning of October 18, Lee wrote a note to the insurgents demanding their surrender; the message was delivered by Stuart. At the same time he wrote the note, Lee instructed the Marines that if the note was refused, they were to be ready to storm the Engine House. He personally instructed the Marines in a quick, off-the-cuff manner about how to tell insurgents from hostages. He also told them to use only bayonets, so wildly fired shots would not hurt the hostages. He specifically ordered them not to harm the slaves inside, as they had been taken as hostages.

While Stuart was talking to Brown (and getting nowhere in his negotiations), someone called out from the Engine House: "Shoot them!" Lee recognized the voice as that of a relative, Lewis W. Washington, whom he now knew was a hostage; Lewis Washington was a descendant of George Washington. Upon hearing Washington's defiant tone, Lee remarked dryly, "The old revolutionary blood does tell."

When negotiations failed, the Marines stormed the Engine House and wounded several of the insurgents. As Lee had instructed, none of the hostages, including the slaves, were harmed.

Lee returned to Harpers Ferry with some troops on the day Brown was executed, as there were rumors that abolitionists would try to fee him. No one appeared.

Lee never made much of John Brown's raid. Though historians count it as one of the foreshadowing acts of the war to follow, Lee considered it just another action of his military career. He apparently never addressed Brown directly or discussed slavery with him.

The Armorer's House, where Lee planned his strategy (and where he was entertained after the tense affair), and the Engine House are both located on Shenandoah Street. Note that the Engine House has been moved about 100 yards from its original location.

Boteler's Ford (Pack Horse Ford)

The ford is located near Shepherdstown. From the downtown area, drive east on West German Street (CR 17), which will start curving down to the Potomac River. About two miles from downtown, you will reach a historic marker at a shallow point in the river.

This is where Lee and the bulk of his army recrossed into western Virginia around midnight on September 19, 1862, after fighting the

Army of the Potomac to a draw at Sharpsburg on September 17. They had originally crossed into Maryland about 30 miles south at White's Ford, near Leesburg. After having crossed the river singing the pro-Confederate "Maryland, My Maryland" that first time, they retired glumly back across the Potomac at Boteler's Ford without saying much at all. Lee himself rode Traveller into the shallow water here and acted as a traffic cop for the wagon train coming across the river. He stayed at that post until the commander of the last division across reported that only a few wagons loaded with wounded and a single battery of cannons were behind him. Lee said, "Thank God," then rode away.

Lee slept somewhere within a mile or so of the ford on the hills above the river. That night, some Federals also crossed the river, and there was a swift, sharp battle fought here. Lee anxiously waited for the outcome. He was told that all of his reserve artillery had been captured and that the Federals were attacking in full force. Not ready to do battle, Lee feared the war could be lost right here on the banks of the Potomac. General A. P. Hill's corps rushed to the river and beat back the Federal detachment that had crossed. The rumor of a full-scale Union assault proved to be false. Lee was relieved.

Bunker Hill

This town is on US 11 about 15 miles west of Harpers Ferry. The Boyd House is now a wedding-oriented bed-and-breakfast that is open only to registered guests.

In early fall 1862, Stonewall Jackson preferred a number of charges against A. P. Hill, calling into question Hill's ability to lead his men.

The Boyd House, where Lee met with Jackson in an effort to mediate Jackson's dispute with A.P. Hill.

After the Battle of Sharpsburg, Jackson was willing to forget the charges, but Hill, insulted that they had been made in the first place, insisted on a court-martial. Lee rode to Jackson's headquarters at the Boyd House in Bunker Hill in October 1862 and tried to mediate the dispute between two of his favorite generals.

Lee failed, just as he had in trying to mediate the dispute between John Floyd and Henry Wise in western Virginia in October 1861. No matter what Lee, their commanding general, said or offered, neither Jackson nor Hill was willing to back down and apologize to the other. Lee finally threw up his hands and walked out of Jackson's headquarters. From that moment until Jackson's death, Jackson and Hill barely spoke to each other, and never in friendly terms. Lee thus showed again that, while he could inspire common soldiers to love him and follow him to their death, he could not always get his immediate subordinates to like or even cooperate with each other.

Cheat Summit Fort/
Valley Mountain/Elkwater

Cheat Summit Fort is on US 250 about 11 miles southeast of Huttonsville. Marked by a turnoff sign, it is reached by driving up a gravel road maintained by the United States Forest Service. The fort has walking trails and interpretive signs. It is open during daylight hours. There is no charge. Valley Mountain, now called Mingo Flats, is located on CR 51 off US 219 about 18 miles south of Huttonsville. Elkwater is on US 219 about 6.8 miles south of Huttonsville.

Once he left Cheat Mountain in September 1861, Lee never returned. That is no surprise. He was mightily embarrassed by his humiliating defeat at this never-to-be battlefield.

In September 1861, Cheat Summit Pass, located along the vital

Valley Mountain, where Lee began to grow his famous white beard

Staunton-Parkersburg Turnpike (today's US 250), was captured by the Federals. By controlling the pass and the road, Union forces controlled the movement of Confederate troops as they passed through the Allegheny and Greenbriar Mountains into western Virginia. If the Federals could keep the Confederates from coming through the pass, they could control their own movements west of the mountains. And if the Federals could mount a large enough force, they might even be able to thrust into the Shenandoah Valley and capture Staunton, a vital railroad town.

Lee arrived with orders to figure out a way to wrest the pass back. Following some advice from a commander in the area, he advocated an advance toward Cheat Mountain from the south along a little-used road, not the eastern route along the turnpike, as the Federals would expect.

Advancing from Monterey, Virginia, to Huntersville, West Virginia, Lee faced his first problem: irritated subordinates. The general in direct command, W. W. Loring, resented his commanding officer's coming into the field to personally supervise the upcoming campaign. Lee also encountered rain like he had never seen; it rained every day for nearly three weeks.

Instead of ordering Loring to move directly against Cheat Mountain, Lee tried to gently persuade him. Though certainly not in the officer's handbook, that technique likely reflected Lee's personal style and his still-developing sense of how to command subordinates.

Lee moved his headquarters in the field to Valley Mountain; the statue of a Confederate soldier marks the field where he set up his tent. At Valley Mountain, Lee pondered his problem in getting Loring to move his men. It was also there that he began to grow his famous white beard. It was not because he was trying to make a fashion statement. His wagon, which contained his shaving kit, among other items, had been left behind in Huntersville, and the muddy roads made it impossible to bring it forward. Lee, who had worn a mustache for years, would have a beard for the rest of his life.

Lee did his own scouting, looking for a way to attack Cheat Summit

*Cheat Summit Fort, where a misguided
underling spoiled Lee's surprise attack*

Fort from an unexpected direction. Finally, on August 12, Loring
moved all of his troops to Lee's camp at Valley Mountain. Lee discovered that the commander of Cheat Summit Fort was an old friend,
Captain John J. Reynolds, who had been a professor of philosophy
when Lee was superintendent at West Point. Son Rooney and Reynolds
briefly greeted each other when Rooney tried to get Reynolds to surrender the fort.

Early in September, Lee caught a break. One of his engineers
discovered a path that opened into a mountain meadow higher than
Cheat Summit Fort; access was from the south, a direction from which
the Federals would never expect the Confederates to attack. Though
about half of Lee's 15,000-man force was sick from the constant rain,
he decided to proceed with the attack plan.

On September 12, 1861, all was in place. The lead Confederates
were supposed to sweep down on the Federal fort in a surprise attack,
to be followed by swift reenforcement. Lee waited ... and waited ...
and waited. Finally, he heard gunfire, but it was coming from the
direction opposite Cheat Mountain. And it was not an attacking vol-
ley of fire, but simple random shooting.

Lee started to ride toward the firing, believing that a Federal
patrol must have discovered his men before they could attack.
Before he could move on to the main road (probably what is now

CR 43, southwest of Cheat Summit Fort near the crossing with Becky Creek), a Federal cavalry patrol, attracted by the firing, thundered by. Lee stayed in the woods, catching his breath. It would not do for the Confederate commander to be captured by Federal cavalry. Just as Lee was about to enter the road again, the same patrol came thundering back in the other direction, having stumbled into the advance lines of the attacking Confederates. This was the first of many occasions during the war that the lucky Lee avoided capture, wounding, or death in close encounters with Federal troops.

Since the Federals were now alerted to the secret Confederate advance and the whole column was in disarray, Lee called off the attack.

He later learned why shots were fired before the force reached the fort, and the reason flabbergasted him. The colonel leading the men had captured some Federal pickets, who told him that the fort had more than 4,000 men inside it. (The real figure was 350.) Believing his Union prisoners, the Confederate colonel decided on his own to call off the attack. Since his troops' muskets were wet and dirty, the colonel ordered the men to fire them in order to clean them. It would not be the last time that incompetent underlings would make Lee look bad.

Lee sent his two aides, son Rooney and Lieutenant Colonel John Augustine Washington, to the left to see if there was any hope of coming in on Cheat Mountain from the west. At Elkwater, the two ran into a Federal picket post. Washington, the last private owner of Mount Vernon, was killed. It was the first and only time in the war that Lee suffered the loss of a personal friend and staff member. It was also the first—but not only—time that Lee had to write a letter of condolence to a widow of a man who had served him. Lee later went to the spot where Washington was killed to see the tragic scene for himself. A historical marker stands there today.

What made the Cheat Summit campaign even worse was that the Richmond newspapers followed it closely and predicted before any shooting took place that it would succeed. When it didn't, they condemned Lee.

After leaving Cheat Mountain, Lee headed for another mountain—

Sewell Mountain—where he would encounter another set of incompetent subordinates and more failure.

Sewell Mountain

Sewell Mountain is on US 60 about 16 miles east of its intersection with US 19 and about 20 miles northeast of Fayetteville. Visitors should turn off US 60 on to Cavendish Road at the historical marker, then drive a short distance uphill to a large tree surrounded by an iron fence, the site of Lee's camp in September 1861.

In late September, Lee walked into the dumbest political and military feud of the war between two of the conflict's most incompetent generals. Both John Floyd and Henry Wise were former governors of Virginia, and both were appointed to their posts by Jefferson Davis. Neither had any military experience. Each hated the other and did his best to undermine him, even if it meant their feud would give advantage to the Federals.

Lee likely had not met either of these dunces previously. He did his best to get Floyd and Wise to cooperate with each other, but he couldn't even get them to link their commands. The generals insisted on keeping their commands separate, on different mountains. The situation did not put Lee in a good humor. Once, on this spot, a young lieutenant came up to him and asked who his ordnance officer was. Lee replied, "I find it strange that an officer of this command who has been here for a week would come up to me who has just arrived and ask who his ordnance officer is. This is in keeping with everything else I find here—no order, no organization, nobody

*The site of Lee's camp at Sewell Mountain in
September 1861*

knows where anything is, no one understands his duty!"

The enemy was only a mile away. Lee could see them clearly from his camp, yet he could never get Floyd and Wise to combine their two commands to attack them, or even prepare their own camps for a Federal attack. Luckily, the Federals were apparently in no mood to move.

The standoff between Floyd and Wise ended within a week, when Wise received an order relieving him of direct command and asking that he report back to Richmond. Davis had finally admitted his mistake in putting the two political enemies on the same front.

With Wise gone and W. W. Loring's little contingent finally in place from Cheat Mountain, Lee was able to build a unified force. He hoped the Federals would attack his entrenchments, but they never did. On October 6, 1861, Confederate scouts told Lee that the Federals were gone. All the noise they had been interpreting as Federals getting ready for an attack was really Federals getting ready for a retreat. For the second time in three months, Lee had prepared an army for a battle that never took place.

When the newspapers in Richmond got wind of another Lee debacle, they again questioned his abilities. Lee responded in a letter to his wife: "I am sorry that the movements of our armies cannot keep pace with the expectations of the editors of the papers. I know they can arrange things satisfactory to themselves on paper. I wish they could do so in the field." By the close of the two failed campaigns in western Virginia, Lee was beginning to develop an intense dislike for newspaper editors. Not once in his Civil War career or his five years of postwar life did he grant a newspaperman an interview.

An early cold snap told Lee that winter was coming. He called off any further plans to pursue the Federals. His men were tired, hungry, dirty, wet, and cold. They were not yet an army willing to do anything at his bidding. His men would not develop that devotion to him for another nine months.

Lee returned to Richmond on October 31 and reported to President Davis about the two failed campaigns. He also exacted a promise from the president that none of the generals who had failed him in the field would be publicly censured. Lee's desire to remain a gentleman was still supreme.

White Sulphur Springs

This town is in southern West Virginia near the Virginia border. The Greenbriar Hotel is on US 64 / US 60 at the site once occupied by the Old White Hotel.

Though the mountains of western Virginia did not hold happy memories for Lee, that did not stop him from returning on vacation during his five years of postwar life. Lee's favorite vacation spot, if judged by the amount of time he spent there between 1867 and 1869, was the Old White Hotel in White Sulphur Springs. Today, the famous Greenbriar Hotel sits on nearly the same site; the Old White was situated on what is now the Greenbriar's front lawn at about a 45-degree angle facing the line of surviving cottages.

Lee was not too enthusiastic about going to the Old White in 1867. He told one of his sons that his wife picked it simply because she hoped its healing waters would relieve her crippling arthritis. The Old White was over the mountains from Washington College in Lexington, requiring at least two days of rough riding. Along the way, Lee stopped at a small inn where some young women recognized him. "The man who stood before us, the embodiment of a Lost Cause, was the realized King Arthur. The soul that looked out of his eyes was as honest and fearless as when it first looked on life," wrote one of the women.

Upon their arrival at the Old White, the Lees settled into the Baltimore Cottage, owned by the Harrison family of Baltimore and apparently loaned to the Lees at no cost. The Baltimore Cottage is located on a row of cottages beside the Greenbriar. A sign outside marks it by name, but no historical marker describes its ties to Lee. The grounds of the Greenbriar are open for touring, but the Baltimore Cottage must be rented if visitors want to see what it is like on the inside.

When Lee walked into the main dining room of the hotel to take his dinner on his first night there, everyone in the room—men and women alike—rose out of respect. They remained standing until he was seated. No one said a word, and no one applauded, believing that it would embarrass him, as it certainly would have.

While Mrs. Lee took in the healing springs, Lee rode Traveller nearly every day, often alone with his thoughts. Whatever those thoughts might have been, they weren't self-pitying or malicious. When he heard that Southerners were ostracizing one of the few Northern families visiting the Old White, Lee took it upon himself to seek out the young women who were the ringleaders of the shunning.

The Baltimore Cottage, where Lee and his wife stayed on their visit to White Sulphur Springs in 1867

"When you go home I want you to take a message to your friends," Lee told the startled ladies. "Tell them from me that it is unworthy of them as women, and especially as Christian women, to cherish feelings of resentment against the North. Tell them that it grieves me inexpressibly to know that such a state of things exists, and that I implore them to do their part to heal our country's wounds." After his speech, he walked over to the Northern family, introduced himself, and sat down to engage them in conversation.

Once, a rumor swept the hotel that Grant was coming for a visit. Lee said he would welcome his old adversary.

Almost as soon as Lee arrived at the Old White in the summer of 1868, he inadvertently and unwisely became involved in presidential politics. It was just a few months before the election pitting Grant, the Republican, against Democrat Horatio Seymour. To stir up emotions, the Republicans were charging that the South, with Democratic help, was embarking on a plan to reenslave the blacks.

One day, former Union general William S. Rosecrans, one of the managers of Seymour's campaign, showed up at the Old White looking for Lee. He wanted Lee to sign a letter explaining that the South had no intention of reenslaving blacks. Such a letter from the South's leading icon would prove to Northern voters that the Republicans were engaging in propaganda.

Lee refused to sign such a letter but suggested he could get other former Confederate leaders spending their summer at the hotel to meet with Rosecrans. Lee brought together an array of former Confederates including General P. G. T. Beauregard and Vice President Alexander H. Stephens. In due time, Lee reluctantly agreed to Rosecrans's suggestion that he and the other Confederate leaders sign a letter stating their views on slavery and the war. The so-called White Sulphur Letter was written by a Virginia lawyer and signed by 31 Confederate leaders. It was mailed to Rosecrans, who saw to it that the letter was published in Northern newspapers. In the letter, the Confederates said that the issues of secession and slavery had been settled by the war, but that the people of the South still were without the rights granted to them under the United States Constitution. It stated that the South would not oppress "the negro" but went on to add that the leaders did not believe the race was ready to take part in political decisions. The letter concluded by promising that the South would "treat the negro populations with kindness and humanity and fulfil every duty incumbent on peaceful citizens, loyal to the Constitution of their country."

Rosecrans was not finished with Lee. He tried to get him to campaign for the Democrats, but Lee refused. Lee seems to have regretted signing the letter. "I did not intend to connect myself with the political questions of the country," he wrote Rosecrans.

Rosecrans's ploy to show that the South was loyal to the United States went unrewarded. Grant was elected in 1868.

Lee came to the Old White for a short season in 1869. It was then that he posed for a photograph with a number of wealthy benefactors and former Confederate generals. Lee was uncomfortable in the photograph, but he realized that being cordial to the wealthy was one of the ways college presidents solicited funds. Historians speculate that the group shot was taken at a spot now occupied by the Greenbriar's tennis courts, as mountains can be seen in the distance.

West Point

The home of the United States Military Academy, West Point is on the west bank of the Hudson River about 40 miles north of New York City. Bus tours are available; a small museum is open daily. For more information, call the visitor center at 845-938-2638 or the museum at 845-938-2703.

It was at the United States Military Academy at West Point where Lee learned to be a soldier. The West Point Museum has a modest display on Lee, including the second portrait of him, done by a man who taught drawing at the academy. The portrait shows a mustached, middle-aged man with a receding hairline. One curiosity about the West Point Museum is that it does not credit Lee with establishing the shako, the familiar feather-plumed hat cadets wear on parade. The museum at Washington and Lee University in Lexington, Virginia, does acknowledge him as the creator of the distinctive hat.

When 18-year-old Robert E. Lee first set foot on the grounds of the United States Military Academy in June 1825, the school had been in existence for 23 years and had been an important military outpost since the American Revolution. He spent four years here making friends

Lee's class raised money to erect a statue to Thaddeus Kosciuszko. The pedestal went up the year before Lee graduated. The statue did not go on the base until 1913.

with young men like fellow Virginian Joseph E. Johnston. Lee shone at West Point, finishing the whole four years without a single demerit and earning second place in his class.

It is almost impossible to imagine Lee's life here as a cadet, as little remains from that time period. None of the wooden barracks or classrooms Cadet Lee used still stand. One West Point relic from Lee's era that does survive is the base pedestal of the statue of Thaddeus Kosciuszko, a Polish artillery officer who fought for the Colonials before coming to West Point in 1778 to construct the first of the fortifications here. Lee's class raised money to erect a statue to the man who first recognized the strategic importance of West Point. The pedestal went up in 1828, the year before Lee graduated. The statue itself did not go on the base until 1913. It has looked out over the strategic bend in the Hudson River ever since.

A bit more remains from Lee's tenure here as superintendent between 1852 and 1855. Portions of the stone barracks that currently stand were built during Lee's tenure as superintendent, but they are off-limits to visitors. The office he used no longer stands. The Old Cadet Chapel, completed in 1837 and located outside West Point's cemetery, is the only building Lee used that is accessible to visitors. He walked here to services from Quarters 100 (the superintendent's house), which still stands on "the Plain" (the parade ground); the house is not open to the public. The walls of the chapel are covered with plaques, most of them dedicated to soldiers who fought and died during the Mexican War. Buried behind the chapel are many notable soldiers, among them Union general John Buford, the cavalry brigade commander who slowed Lee's advance on Gettysburg just enough to give the Union army time to concentrate its forces, and Lieutenant Alonzo Cushing, who died defending his cannon battery when it became the focal point of Lee's third-day assault at Gettysburg.

In the three years Lee served as superintendent, 24 graduates passed through who went on to become Union generals and 14 who went on to become Confederate generals, including his son Custis and nephew Fitzhugh. For the South, there were John Bell Hood, John Pegram, and J. E. B. Stuart, among others. Among those who served the North were Philip Sheridan, Oliver O. Howard, and Stephen H. Weed.

Though Lee brought some innovations to the curriculum, such as

The Old Cadet Chapel is the only building Lee used that is accessible to visitors.

Lee would walk from Quarters 100 (the superintendent's house) to services at the Old Cadet Chapel.

requiring cadets to learn Spanish, he did not like his service at West Point. He found the rote method of learning antiquated and post life less that what he wanted; he had worked hard to become a military engineer, only to find himself supervising disciplinary hearings. Though it provided him ample time with his family after faraway service in Mexico, he missed the stimulation of doing different things every day.

That changed in 1855, when the secretary of war pushed through Congress a plan to expand the United States military presence in the West, in order to protect settlers pushing toward the Pacific from increasing threats from Indians. Two new regiments of cavalry, including the Second United States Cavalry, were created. Albert Sidney Johnston was appointed colonel and, for reasons that are still unclear, engineer Robert E. Lee was appointed lieutenant colonel. The secretary of war was Jefferson Davis. Lee was puzzled at the appointment. He was a military engineer who had never commanded men in the field during his entire 26 years in the army. Now, he was second in command of a cavalry regiment. Lee did not question the assignment, as he firmly believed in duty. He left West Point on April 12, 1855, bound for Louisville, Kentucky, to take over command of the cavalrymen.

Fort Hamilton

What is left of Fort Hamilton is virtually underneath the eastern terminus of the Verrazano Narrows Bridge on I-278 West. To reach the fort from Manhattan by subway, take the R train to the end of the line at 95th Street in Brooklyn and walk south toward the bridge. After reaching a little public park featuring a huge Civil War-era cannon, turn left and walk toward the 100th Street entrance to the fort. Be prepared to show photo identification to the guard, as this is an active military base. Take the first street to the right and walk one block to the Harbor Defense Museum. Admission to the museum is free. Call 718-630-4349 for details. St. John's Episcopal Church is located a couple of blocks away at the intersection of Fort Hamilton Parkway and 99th Street.

It is hard to think of a man so closely associated with the South living in Brooklyn and riding his horse down Broadway in Manhattan, but Robert E. Lee was stationed at Fort Hamilton in 1840. Lee's duty was to improve the defenses of New York Harbor, an assignment that covered four different forts on both sides of the narrows. One fort, Lafayette, was located directly in front of Hamilton but was destroyed when the bridge was constructed.

Fort Hamilton was 10 years old when Lee was assigned here, but it was already showing its age. One of Lee's first responsibilities was waterproofing the fort's walls to keep water from flowing into the casemates on the first floor. Later, he extended the walls in order to mount more cannons to protect the harbor.

Among the officers stationed at Fort Hamilton during Lee's tenure

What is left of Fort Hamilton is virtually underneath the eastern terminus of the Verrazano Narrows Bridge.

were Captain Erasmus Keys, Lieutenant John Sedgwick, and Lieutenant Henry Hunt, all men who would become Union generals in the 1860s. It was Hunt's cannons that destroyed Lee's third-day assault at Gettysburg. Sedgwick fell dead from a sniper under Lee's command during the Battle of Spotsylvania Court House in 1864.

It was while stationed at Fort Hamilton that Lee developed one of his closest relationships—with a dog.

One day, Lee rescued a female terrier from the narrows off Fort Hamilton. He named her Dart. In time, she had a litter of puppies, and Lee kept a lively little black-and-tan, which he named Spec.

Spec came to think of himself as part of the family. On Sundays, the Lees would walk to nearby St. John's Episcopal Church, leaving Spec closed inside the house. Spec soon learned he could jump out a second-story window and beat the family to church. The church had a very understanding priest, who finally allowed Spec to worship with the family.

Spec may have been the family dog, but he was devoted to Lee. "I catch him sometimes sitting up and looking at me so intently that I am for a moment startled," Lee wrote in a letter to Mary, describing how lonely it was for master and dog to be at Fort Hamilton while the family was visiting Arlington.

Robert Jr.'s remembrance of Spec was captured in a biography he wrote of his father. He told of the dog's first glimpse of Lee after he had been fighting in Mexico for more than two years: "Spec's extravagance of his demonstrations of delight left no doubt that he knew at once his kind master and loving friend."

Spec disappeared during the family's residence in Baltimore while Lee was working on Fort Carroll. The future general who would later send men to their deaths in battle was heartbroken over the loss of his constant companion.

The Harbor Defense Museum at Fort Hamilton is located in a unique structure called a carporiner, a small, triangular, fully enclosed fort. One point of the triangle faces the land side. This design would force attacking enemy troops to split on either side of the carporiner. Once the enemies reached the outer wall of Fort Hamilton, they would be forced into a deep ditch, where soldiers inside both Fort Hamilton and the carporiner could fire on them like fish in a barrel. Luckily for those men, no one ever attacked Fort Hamilton. The museum has a display on Lieutenant Lee's service at the fort, including a mannequin in an 1841 uniform.

The remaining part of the original fort where Lee served is directly in front of the museum. The second floor, once the parapet where the cannons were mounted, is now enclosed; it serves as an officers' club open only to military members. Visitors to the museum can walk to one of the remaining outer walls of the fort for a good view of the bridge and the narrows.

Before leaving Fort Hamilton, head back toward the main entrance but turn right before exiting and walk half a block into the post. From the entrance, the first white house on the left is the Lee House. Post historians are unsure if it is the original house in which Lee and his family lived from 1841 to 1846, but they believe that the house at least rests on the site the Lees inhabited. It was in the house at Fort Hamilton that Margaret Childe, the fourth daughter and seventh and last child of the Lees, was conceived; she was born in Arlington.

There was once a barn behind the house where, in 1845, eight-year-old Rooney accidentally chopped off the tips of two fingers. Lee sat up several nights in a row to hold the boy's hands so he would not pull out the stitches.

When you are ready to leave Fort Hamilton, you may want to walk to nearby St. John's Episcopal Church, at Fort Hamilton Parkway and 99th Street. This is where Lee served as vestryman during his tour of duty and where future general Thomas J. "Stonewall" Jackson was baptized as a Christian when he was stationed here in 1849. It was to this church that Spec would run and wait on the steps for the Lees.

The baptismal font used by the priest who baptized Jackson is on display inside the church, which is generally open after nine in the morning. It has changed much since 1842, thanks mostly to a fire several years ago. Still, two of the stained-glass windows that were in place during Lee's time at the church survive. In the front yard is a plaque on a tree planted by the United Daughters of the Confederacy; it replaced a tree planted by Lee.

Oddly enough, an incident that took place at this church offers a very rare look at Lee's bawdy side. In the mid-1840s, the Episcopal Church was embroiled in a dispute involving Bishop Edward Pusey, whose vision of the "high church"—sometimes called "Puseyism"—placed a heavy emphasis on the literal belief in the Eucharist as the body of Christ. Other Episcopalians favored the "low church" belief that Communion should be viewed as strictly symbolic of Christ's sacrifice. Lee was a believer in the low church, not caring for increased ritual. During one particularly heated meeting of the church vestry, Lee turned to fellow officer Henry Hunt, a future Union general, and whispered, "Beware of Pussyism! Pussyism is always bad, and may lead to unChristian feeling; therefore beware of Pussyism!" He intentionally mispronounced the bishop's name to give it a sexual connotation.

Chambersburg

This town is in south-central Pennsylvania about 15 miles above the Maryland line; it is accessible via US 30, US 11, and I-81.

One site of interest to visitors is the public square in downtown Chambersburg, now dominated by a statue of a dangerously casual soldier (whose wrist is resting over the muzzle of a cocked and presumably loaded musket). It was here on June 26, 1863, that Robert E. Lee first came in close contact with a curious Northern public. It was also here where what might have been one of the great photographs of the war went untaken. Alerted that Lee was coming to the square, citizens began to gather. An enterprising photographer set himself up in the second-floor window of a building, intending to take the general's photograph. But too many citizens and soldiers started to crowd his view, and the photographer gave up, as the six-second exposure time would have blurred everyone. That photograph would have been the only one ever taken of Lee in the field in the North.

It was also in Chambersburg that Lee reissued orders to calm nervous shopkeepers. The orders read in part, "No greater disgrace could befall the army, and through it our own people, than the perpetration of the barbarous outrages upon the unarmed and defenseless and the wanton destruction of private property, that have marked the course of the enemy in our own country. It must be remembered that we make war only upon armed men."

About the only things the Confederates took while they were in Pennsylvania were hats. Bareheaded soldiers would snatch them off the heads of curious civilians standing by the side of the road. Officers tried to stop the practice, but few hats were returned to their owners. Curiously, even one of Lee's personal friends, General Henry Heth, succumbed to the practice, but it saved his life. On July 1, wearing a new, oversized hat stuffed with newspapers to make it fit, Heth was shot in the head. The wadded newspapers slowed the bullet enough to save his life.

Still in Chambersburg but east of the downtown area on US 30 is a historical marker noting the site of the tent headquarters that Lee set up in the woods on the first night he was in town; that area is now a neighborhood. It was in the campsite on June 28 that Lee listened to a scout named Harrison tell him that General George Meade was now in command of the Army of the Potomac and that it was marching north to engage the Confederates. Harrison's report frightened Lee. If true, it meant that the Federals knew he had invaded the North. Worse, Lee had not heard any direct word of warning about the Union movement from J. E. B. Stuart, who had been told to keep him informed. It was from here that Lee, fearful that he was about to face a large, unified Union army, issued orders to his far-flung command to concentrate at Gettysburg.

Cashtown

This community lies about 15 miles east of Chambersburg via Old US 30 off US 30. Less than four miles west of Cashtown are signs for Old US 30. This is the original Chambersburg Pike, which Lee and part of the Army of Northern Virginia took to reach Gettysburg.

The Cashtown Inn is the hotel that was the temporary headquarters of General A. P. Hill. It was from here that Hill gave his fateful, casual approval to General Henry Heth to go ahead and scout Gettysburg on July 1. The purpose of Heth's foray was to check into the existence of a rumored storehouse of shoes. Lee had given express orders to his generals not to go into Gettysburg in force until all his army was concentrated. Heth went on his "scouting" mission with a full division, a force many times larger than Lee would have approved.

Lee spent the night of June 30 on the road to Gettysburg pondering a report delivered to him from A. P. Hill at the Cashtown Inn that a brigade of North Carolinians had seen Federal cavalry late that afternoon west of Gettysburg. If true, it meant the Federals might already be concentrating in the town.

It was somewhere west of Cashtown on the morning of July 1 that Lee heard the rumble of cannon fire. Alarmed that a battle he had not ordered was under way, he spurred Traveller faster toward Cashtown. There, he demanded that A. P. Hill inform him what was happening. Hill, who had no idea, mounted and rode east to find out, while Lee likely rested on the porch of the Cashtown Inn.

It was here that Lee was heard to say, "I cannot think what has become of Stuart. I ought to have heard from him long before now. I am in ignorance as to what we have in front of us here. If it is the whole Federal force, we must fight a battle here." Without waiting for Hill's return, Lee left the inn and started riding toward the sound of the guns. He reached a hill—perhaps what is now known as Herr's Ridge, much of which has been lost to a housing development—from which he first saw the ground west of Gettysburg and the high ground east of the town. For the rest of July 1, Lee stayed in the saddle, moving along his lines and closer to Gettysburg. By the end of the day, he was almost at its outskirts.

Gettysburg

Gettysburg, 10 miles southeast of Cashtown, is reached by US 30, US 15, PA 34, and PA 116. Gettysburg National Military Park and its famous sites—the Peach Orchard, the Wheatfield, Little Round Top, Seminary Ridge, Cemetery Ridge—lie south of the downtown area. Admission to the park is free, though there is a charge for a few of its attractions; call 717-334-1124 for information.

Gettysburg, the best-known battle of the war and the scene of Lee's greatest defeat, had no strategic significance as a town. The only reason Lee and his army arrived there on the morning of July 1, 1863, was that he had received word from a spy visiting his camp in Chambersburg that the Army of the Potomac had discovered the Confederates' crossing of the Potomac. Lee had envisioned capturing Pennsylvania's capital, Harrisburg, and was just 30 miles away when the spy told him that the Federals were rushing to attack. Looking at a map for a place to concentrate his army—which had split into several parts to scour the countryside for supplies—he noticed that five different roads led to Gettysburg, making it a natural rendezvous point. Lee had brought his army north for several reasons. Two years of war had exhausted the South of food and livestock, while the North remained virtually untouched; it was a breadbasket of supplies just a few days' march north of devastated Virginia. Lee's army was at its strongest, coming off victories at Fredericksburg six months earlier and Chancellorsville just two months earlier. Lee and the Confederate high command believed that a victory on Northern soil might create a collapse in civilian support for the war and a public demand that Lincoln let the South go its own way. And lastly, the government in Richmond hoped that a decisive Southern victory would bring official recognition and financial help from England and France.

Lee gave explicit orders to all his generals to avoid any small battles that would tip the Federals to his location. One general, Henry Heth, ignored that order by attacking a Union force west of Gettysburg early on the morning of July 1, hours before the portion of the army traveling with Lee east from Chambersburg arrived, and still longer before the portion coming with General Richard Ewell could arrive from the north.

Forced into a general battle before the army was "up," or concentrated, Lee's men did well under the circumstances, finally driving the Federals through town. But that turned out to be a bad thing, since those Federals retreated to higher, better ground south of Gettysburg. Ewell, having taken over corps command after Stonewall Jackson's death, chased the Federals to the base of the high ground but then stopped as night fell. Subordinate generals grumbled that Jackson would have charged right up the hill. Had Ewell succeeded in storming the hill, the Confederates would have had the high ground that defined the battle for the next two days.

On July 2, Lee ordered an attack on the far left Union flank. His second in command, James Longstreet, repeatedly suggested to Lee that they withdraw from the field. Longstreet did not get his men in place to attack the Federal flank until hours later than Lee had ordered.

About 12,000 men from seven Southern states, under the command of Pettigrew, Pickett, and Trimble, marched from the woods on Seminary Ridge toward the Federals on Cemetery Ridge.

That delay gave the Federals time to concentrate along Cemetery Ridge, which ended at the Round Tops, two hills that commanded the landscape along the Union line. All during that afternoon, fierce battles were fought on peaceful-sounding ground—Little Round Top, the Peach Orchard, and the Wheatfield. Once, for a brief few minutes, Confederates broke through the center of the Federal line on Cemetery Ridge, but the unsupported troops had to retreat.

On July 3, Lee felt he had no choice but to attack the Union center. Historians still debate what made him think his men could march across a mile of open ground into the face of Union cannons and muskets. It likely was nothing more complicated than a belief that the same men who had defeated an army twice their size at Chancellorsville could do the same at Gettysburg. Lee believed the Federals had reenforced both ends of the line and so were weak in the center.

At one o'clock in the afternoon that day, scores of Confederate cannons began to bombard the Union lines in hopes that the shelling would either destroy the troops or drive them away from the wall on Cemetery Ridge. At three o'clock, about 12,000 men from seven Southern states under the command of three generals—James Johnston Pettigrew, George Pickett, and Isaac Trimble—started marching from the woods on Seminary Ridge toward the Federals on Cemetery Ridge. The Pettigrew-Pickett-Trimble Assault (misnamed by Virginia newspapers as "Pickett's Charge") lasted less than an hour. A handful of North Carolinians and Virginians broke through the Federal lines behind a stone wall near a small clump of trees. Altogether, about 7,000 men—more than half the force that started out—were killed, wounded, or captured.

Lee, who had watched the assault move out, now saw his broken command return. As he rode out to meet his men, they rallied to his side, telling him that they would re-form and try again. Lee sadly shook his head. The fighting for Gettysburg was over.

George Meade, the Union general, refused Lincoln's demand that he move his army forward to crush the crippled Confederates. Within 10 days after Gettysburg, Lee's Army of Northern Virginia was safely back across the Potomac River. It would rest and refit and be back in fighting form by the fall.

One Lee site in Gettysburg is the small stone house that now serves as General Lee's Museum and Gift Shop, located on the western edge of the town. Lee went to bed here after midnight on July 1. This may be the same stone house to which the body of General John Reynolds, commander of the Union's First Corps, was taken after he was killed that morning. (This was not the same John Reynolds who was a friend of Lee's when he was superintendent at West Point.) Lee apparently did not use the stone house as his headquarters during his four days in Gettysburg. Reports indicate that he operated mostly from his tent, set up in a field across the road from the house. The field has a marker.

It was to this field that Lee returned after midnight on July 4, after riding from one of his generals' headquarters to another. Few members of his staff were awake. According to witnesses, Lee could barely dismount. Someone was startled to hear Lee cry, "Too bad, oh, too bad!" That was his comment on the attack he had seen fail earlier that day.

Travelers will likely want to visit the National Park Service visitor center at Gettysburg National Military Park to obtain a map of the battlefield. The Lee statue on Confederate Avenue looking east toward Cemetery Ridge depicts the general watching the Pettigrew-Pickett-Trimble Assault. According to reports, when the attack failed, he rode forward from this point to meet his men. Seeing a dazed Pickett returning from the field, Lee urged him to see to his division. Pickett replied that he had no division.

Hardy visitors can walk from the Lee statue all the way to Cemetery Ridge, a distance of about a mile.

Fort Carroll

This abandoned fort is best seen by looking east from the Francis Scott Key Bridge on I-695 heading north from Baltimore. The only way to get a close look is by small boat. The cruise boat from Baltimore's inner harbor stops before going under the Francis Scott Key Bridge, but it does offer a distant glimpse of the fort.

Maryland is home to an irreplaceable relic that is literally falling apart—Fort Carroll, the only fort designed and built by Robert E. Lee.

When Lee returned from Mexico in June 1848 after nearly two years of war, he was ready for a new challenge. He got it when he was assigned to come up with the design of a fort to replace Fort McHenry on the Patapsco River. True, Fort McHenry had protected Baltimore in the War of 1812, but now both the city and the military felt a fort farther distant was justified.

Lee began work in the spring of 1849 at Sollers' Point Flats, a shoal in the middle of the river. The spot selected for the fort (not by Lee himself) presented interesting engineering challenges. Most forts, with the exception of Forts Jefferson, Sumter, and Wool, were on dry land, not on sand bars. Lee had to determine how far down into the river bottom he must drive piles in order to support the foundation, then how much rock it would take to create that foundation. He also had to design heavy-duty equipment to build the fort, such as a pile driver and a crane. He even had to come up with his own methods of construction, which included experimenting with pouring concrete under water.

Work on the fort progressed through the summer of 1852. The walls were rising when Lee was surprised with a letter out of the blue; he was being assigned to the superintendency of the United States Military Academy at West Point. Actually, he was more than surprised. He was shocked. Lee had been a field engineer and staff officer for nearly 23 years. He knew absolutely nothing about running a college for the military. He wrote a letter to the secretary of war asking that the appointment be reconsidered and that he be left in place at Fort Carroll. The secretary refused. His more than three years of living and working in Baltimore notwithstanding, Lee was to report to West Point.

Fort Carroll, designed to have three tiers of casements like Fort Sumter, was never finished as originally designed. The Patapsco River proved too much of a challenge, even for an engineer like Lee. Within 10 years of the time he started the foundation, the fort began to sink into the mud. Later engineers decided not to add to the weight by building more casements. The fort was never fully occupied. By 1862, it was obsolete anyway, as proven by the attack on similarly designed Fort Pulaski outside Savannah, Georgia.

Did Lee make a mistake in his engineering calculations? Probably not. He did not select the site on a mud flat and likely would not have put the fort there by his own choice. He had seen what water could do when he was engineering the Mississippi and examining water damage to forts in North Carolina. In 1848, anyone's engineering skills were limited by what they could see. The bottom of the river was 48 feet down, and Lee had no way to examine conditions at that depth.

Over the years, there have been efforts to save the only fort designed by Lee, but so far, nothing has been done.

Lee returned to Baltimore after the Civil War to visit friends and attend board meetings of a company that was looking into extending a railroad into Virginia. However, none of the houses, buildings, or churches he visited seems to have survived.

Sharpsburg

The town is located at the junction of MD 65 and MD 34 about 10 miles south of Hagerstown and just a couple of miles east of the Potomac River and the West Virginia border. Antietam National Park curves around Sharpsburg. A fee is charged; call 301-432-5124 for information. Antietam Creek is east of town.

Like Gettysburg, which would come nine months later, the Battle of Sharpsburg (called Antietam by the North) took place where it did because of circumstances that were beyond Lee's control.

Lee intended to pass through Maryland in September 1862, picking up recruits for his 40,000-man army before carrying the war into Pennsylvania (much as he would try again during the Gettysburg Campaign). But before Lee reached Pennsylvania, he had to neutralize the Federal garrison at Harpers Ferry in western Virginia. He split his army into four pieces and sent three of those pieces under Stonewall Jackson toward Harpers Ferry.

A copy of the order outlining this strategy was accidentally dropped in a field near Frederick, Maryland, as Lee's army passed. It was found by a Union soldier and taken to the commanding general of the Army of the Potomac, George McClellan, who subsequently began a pursuit, though a slow one.

A Southern sympathizer happened to be in McClellan's camp when the order was delivered. He rushed to Lee with the news that his battle plan had been discovered. Since his army was now scattered over more than 20 miles and the Federals were on their way, Lee knew it was too late to continue his Northern invasion, and maybe too late to recross the Potomac. He had no choice but to stop in his tracks and hope that Stonewall Jackson could reach him near Sharpsburg.

Lee's plan was simple. He would wait along Antietam Creek for the parts of his army coming from Harpers Ferry and South Mountain to join him. Thanks to McClellan's caution and his belief that Lee's army was larger than his own (it was actually only half the size), the battle did not start for two days, time that Lee used to gather his strength.

The Battle of Sharpsburg opened at dawn on September 17, 1862, as Federal regiments rushed across Miller's Corn Field toward Confederates holding the West Woods. Those two areas traded hands several times in bloody charges during the morning, before the Union finally pulled back.

When the fighting for Miller's Corn Field died down, the battle shifted to the center near the Sunken Road, a farm lane that had dropped below the land's natural grade due to decades of wagon traffic. For three hours, Federals attacked the Sunken Road, which would later be dubbed "Bloody Lane." The Confederates were finally dislodged, but McClellan, fearing that Lee had pulled his men out of line as some sort of trick, refused to rush reserves into the gap.

Now, the fighting shifted to the Confederate right flank near a stone bridge later dubbed "Burnside's Bridge" for Union general Ambrose Burnside, who would spend several hours trying to capture a bridge over a stream that was barely knee-deep. A few hundred Georgians dug into the hillside above the bridge kept an entire Union

Lee's headquarters at Sharpsburg is now a small, shaded lot with a monument marking the spot.

corps pinned down for much of the afternoon.

Finally forcing their way across the bridge, the Federals advanced on the weakened Confederates. None of their officers paid much attention to a blue-clad column rushing toward them from the south, apparently believing they were reenforcements—even though the men were coming from the wrong direction. The mystery column turned out to be the Light Division under Confederate general A. P. Hill. They were not attempting to disguise themselves, but were rather wearing captured Union overcoats because it was the simplest way to carry them. Hill's men poured a devastating fire into the Union flank, crippling what would have been an almost certain Union attack, had they not arrived when they did.

McClellan pulled his army back, never even engaging the tens of thousands of men he held in reserve, out of fear that Lee, too, had a reserve force. Lee carefully pulled his army back across the Potomac, comfortable in the knowledge that he would one day in the future carry the war to the North.

Lee's headquarters for the battle is now a small, shaded lot on the north side of MD 34 about a half-mile west of downtown Sharpsburg. A monument marks the spot. It was here that Lee received a message from Stonewall Jackson that Harpers Ferry had been captured. And it was here that he formulated his bold strategy based on what he knew about McClellan. Lee had beaten McClellan just three months earlier during the Seven Days. He understood that McClellan was too cautious to attack before everything was perfectly in order. That gave Lee time to put his army together. And it was at this headquarters that Lee was first heard to give a nickname to Longstreet. After the battle, all the Confederate generals gathered in this field to give their reports. Longstreet was late, and Lee began to worry that something had happened to him. At last, Longstreet rode up. Lee shook his hand, saying, "Here is Longstreet, my old war horse."

It was not far north of his headquarters that Lee experienced one of his many close calls during the war. While conferring with Longstreet and D. H. Hill over what to do about an expected Federal counterattack through Miller's Corn Field and into the West Woods, the three generals rode up to a little hill to see what they could see. Lee and Longstreet both dismounted, while Hill stayed on his horse. Longstreet joked that Hill would get them all killed by presenting himself as a target for Federal artillery. Hill ignored the warning. As he watched a Federal battery through his binoculars and noted a puff of smoke, Longsteet said to Hill, "There is a shot for you." Seconds later, a cannonball took off the legs of Hill's horse. All three generals were unhurt.

Warrenton

> The town is located at the junction of US 401 and NC 58 in north-central North Carolina, not far below the Virginia line. To reach Annie Lee's grave, drive about 9.5 miles south from town on US 401, then turn right on SR 1137 (Annie Lee Road). After 0.2 mile, pull left into the parking lot for the cemetery. Annie's grave was originally under the obelisk.

Though General Robert E. Lee loved his North Carolina troops— even going so far as to bestow the nickname "Tar Heels" for the way they stood their ground in the face of the enemy—the state itself held only sadness.

Lee's second daughter, Annie, was born with a wine-stain birthmark on her face. As a child, she had an accident with a pair of scissors that gashed her eye. The two disfigurements only made her more endearing to her father, who wanted to make sure she did not let her appearance keep her from doing what she wanted.

Apparently, Annie took the Lee spirit to heart. As she grew, she became one of the leaders among the Lee sisters and learned much about the business of running a household and a plantation.

In August 1862, Annie and two of her sisters, Agnes and Mildred, accompanied their sister-in-law Charlotte Lee (Rooney's wife) to Jones Springs, North Carolina, a sulphur-springs resort about 10 miles south of Warrenton. Though the family hoped that Charlotte's baby son, Rob, would be healed from his sickness, little Robert died at the springs. Annie and Agnes decided to stay on there after his death.

In early October, Annie came down with an illness that was likely typhoid fever. Mrs. Lee rushed down from Arlington to be by her side. Annie lingered before dying on October 20, 1862. She was 23, the only child of the Lees to die before the parents.

Lee was then with his army around Culpeper in Virginia, trying to recover from the Battle of Sharpsburg in September. He received notice of her death but was unable to leave the army to attend her burial or even visit the grave.

For reasons unknown, Lee did not visit his daughter's grave immediately after the war, when he was in relatively good health and living relatively close (Richmond). It was not until 1870, when his health was failing and when the trustees of Washington College ordered him to take time off from his duties as college president, that Lee decided to find Annie's grave. He sensed that his own time on earth was coming to an end. In one letter to son Rooney, he wrote, "I have always promised myself to go there and I think if I am to accomplish it, I have no time to lose."

On March 28, 1870, Lee and Agnes spent the night at the home of John J. White at the corner of Marshall and Eaton Streets in Warrenton. The next morning, they borrowed a carriage from the Whites and drove to the little cemetery where Annie rested. They left a bouquet of hyacinths.

Lee wrote his wife that "my visit to Annie's grave was mournful yet soothing to my feelings and I was glad to have the opportunity of thanking the kind friends for their care of her while living and their attention to her since her death."

Lee subsequently boarded a train in Warrenton to continue his

Lee and his daughter Agnes visited Annie's gravesite near Warrenton in March 1870.

Southern tour. He passed through Raleigh, Salisbury, and Charlotte as old soldiers lined the stations.

On the return journey, Lee stopped in Wilmington and spent one night at the home of George Davis, who had been attorney general of the Confederacy. He left the next day. The house, near downtown on Market Street, no longer stands.

In 1994, a few fragments of Annie Lee's casket were recovered and transported to Lexington, Virginia. She thus became the last of the Lee family to be entombed at Washington and Lee University.

Lee served only briefly in North Carolina when he conducted a thorough examination of Fort Macon.

Fort Macon

This fort is located at the eastern tip of Bogue Banks, a barrier island accessible via US 70 through Morehead City. Fort Macon is now a North Carolina State Park. Admission is free; call 252-726-3775 for information.

Lee served only briefly in North Carolina. In November 1840, he conducted a thorough examination of Fort Macon. It revealed that the fort was in danger of falling into the Atlantic Ocean due to beach erosion. His solution was the same one he had employed to control the Mississippi River in St. Louis: he recommended building dams to divert the flow of water away from the beaches near the fort.

During that same time, Lee may have gone farther south to visit Fort Caswell, now part of the North Carolina Baptist Convention's meeting center on Oak Island, southwest of Wilmington. Fort Caswell, too, was experiencing erosion problems. It is not easily seen by the public today, unless they are Baptists visiting the center.

Not long after Lee completed his report on Fort Macon, he received orders to report to Fort Hamilton in New York.

Charleston

Located on a narrow peninsula between the Cooper and Ashley Rivers, Charleston is accessible via US 17 from the northeast and the southwest, I-26 from the northwest, and US 52 from the north.

In 1861, Charleston was one of the largest and most important cities in the South, thanks in part to its port. It was an obvious target for Federal capture.

In 1861, Lee spent about a week inspecting Charleston's defenses, including Fort Sumter.

*Edmonston-Alston House Museum, where Lee
and his staff escaped from a great fire that swept
through parts of Charleston*

Lee spent about a week inspecting Charleston's defenses, including Fort Sumter. It was while walking around Fort Sumter before he was famous that a local citizen described him as "the most striking figure we had ever encountered, the figure of a man about 56 or 58 years of age [actually 55], erect as a poplar, yet lithe and graceful, with broad shoulders thrown back, a fine justly-proportioned head posed in unconscious dignity, clear, deep, thoughtful eyes and the quiet, dauntless step of one every inch the gentleman and soldier."

While in Charleston, Lee stayed at the Mills House Hotel. The modern Mills House, located at 115 Meeting Street at the intersection with Queen Street, is a faithful (though taller) reproduction of the original. In December 1861, a great fire swept across Charleston. Lee and other guests watched the fire from the roof of the hotel until shifting winds sent the flames in their direction. Lee grabbed a lady's baby and led the civilians down the rear steps. Luckily, the fire stopped before it reached the hotel. One story, unsubstantiated and likely part of the postwar creation of Lee's legend, has him directing the firefighters' efforts. It is doubtful that professional, civilian firefighters would have taken orders from a stranger in uniform.

To get away from the smoke, Lee and his staff spent a few days at the home of Charles Alston, at 21 East Battery Street. Now operated as the Edmondston-Alston House Museum, it is open to the public; call 843-556-6020 for information.

While in Charleston, Lee encountered someone rare indeed—a man who did not like him. General Roswell Ripley, an Ohioan who had thrown in with the South since he had married a Southerner, did not like Lee telling him how to prepare his coastal defenses. Ripley complained all the way to the South Carolina governor about Lee's being an interloper.

Lee moved between his two headquarters at Coosawhatchie and Charleston until March 1862, when he was ordered to Richmond.

He returned to Charleston in April 1870 on his Southern tour. He spent the night at 60 Montague Street at the home of H. E. Young,

Lee spent the night at 60 Montague Street during his Southern tour in 1870.

a former member of his staff. Two different receptions were held for him, at which bands played. The bands refused to leave until Lee made a short speech. It was the only time during the tour that Lee gave anything approaching a public address. 60 Montague Street is a private home. Please don't trespass. He left Charleston on April 28 without ever visiting Fort Sumter or any of the military installations he had strengthened during his earlier stay in the city.

Coosawhatchie

This village is located at Exit 28 off I-95 about an hour north of Savannah, Georgia.

In the late fall of 1861, Lee was in command of the Department of South Carolina, Georgia, and Florida. His duty was to prepare those states for Federal invasion. Part of his job was to tour the defenses to determine if they could be improved. He started at Coosawhatchie. Barely even a community today, this place was of strategic military importance in 1861, since it lay at the northern head of the Broad River, which runs from Port Royal Sound deep into the interior of South Carolina. The railroad line that crossed the river at Coosawhatchie was considered vital. If Union gunboats could run up the ever-narrowing river and bombard the railroad bridge, it would cripple South Carolina's ability to ship supplies to troops.

Lee based his camp in a local house and started supervising the digging of extensive earthworks along the river (all of which are on private property today) to protect the railroad. To reach the entire line, Lee needed a good horse. He noticed a South Carolina officer in camp whom he had met at Sewell Mountain in western Virginia several weeks earlier. This man was the owner of Greenbriar, a horse Lee had earlier tried to purchase. Lee again offered $200 for the horse. This time, the offer was accepted. Since the horse would be expected to cover a lot of ground on inspection tours, Lee renamed him Traveller. Traveller would remain Lee's primary mount throughout the war. He rode the horse almost daily until 1870, the year of his death. Traveller died seven months later.

There is not much to Coosawhatchie today. Still, it is valuable to see how wide the river is and how close Union gunboats could have run to the railroad bridge.

Savannah

Located near the Atlantic and across the Savannah River from South Carolina, the city is accessible by traveling US 17, I-95, or I-16.

Savannah is about 15 miles west of Cockspur Island, where Lee was assigned to prepare the land for a masonry fort that would become Fort Pulaski. It is not hard to understand why Lee liked Savannah. Trying to come up with an engineering plan to drain enough water to allow a firm foundation for a great fort was hot, lonely work in the swamp. Savannah, a city of 7,000 in 1829, was an oasis complete with clean sheets and warm friendships. Lee stayed in or visited several houses in Savannah. One of these was the home of the Mackays, who lived on Broughton Street between Abercorn and Lincoln; no evidence of the house exists today.

More remains from Lee's trips in early 1862 and April 1870.

A home Lee visited in 1862, when he was inspecting Georgia's coastal defenses, and again in 1870, when he was on his Southern tour, was the Sorrel-Weed House at 6 West Harris Street on Madison Square. This was the boyhood home of Moxley Sorrel, General James

During his Southern tour in 1870, Lee stayed at Andrew Low's house, instead of with his friend Andrew Lawton, in order to fool the adoring crowds.

Longstreet's chief of staff. During the latter visit, Lee and Sorrel had plenty of old stories to share—of combat and of Longstreet. Sorrel was severely wounded four times during the war but nonetheless rose from private to general—not bad for a bank clerk with no military training. The house is privately owned today.

During his well-known 1870 trip, Lee visited the home at 127-131 Lincoln Street. It was here that he met Andrew Lawton, one of his old generals and his former quartermaster. Lee and his host engaged in a bit of subterfuge. Knowing that his guest would attract crowds, General Lawton spirited Lee and daughter Agnes over to Andrew Low's house, located about a dozen blocks away at 329 Abercorn Street, so they could get some undisturbed rest. (Low would one day become the father-in-law of Juliette Gordon Low, the founder of the Girl Scouts.) The ruse worked. A band showed up at the Lawton residence to serenade Lee. General Lawton did not tell them that Lee was not there to hear the music.

On the evening of April 2, 1870, Low hosted a dinner party that must have been something to witness. Among the guests who came to see Lee was General Joseph Johnston, his old classmate and the man Lee replaced as commander of the Army of Northern Virginia after

Johnston was wounded at the Battle of Seven Pines in May 1862. Had Johnston not been wounded, Lee may have never risen to prominence. Back in 1861, Johnston had been irritated when Lee was named a general before him, but he later graciously said that the best thing that ever happened to the South was his wounding. After dinner, Lee broached a subject that was embarrassing to him. Another old Confederate general, Samuel Cooper, had fallen on hard times. Lee asked the dinner party to help him contribute something to send to Cooper. The next morning, Lee and Johnston posed for a joint photograph showing two tired men.

Fort Jackson

This fort is three miles east of downtown Savannah on President Street, reached via US 80. Though privately owned today, the fort is open for touring; call 912-232-3945 for information.

Lee visited Fort Jackson frequently while trying to develop a strategy for the lower coast in late 1861.

One of the oldest forts in the country, Fort Jackson was completed in 1809. It never fired a shot at any enemy ships trying to come up the Savannah River, but it did serve as headquarters for all the other forts in the area. Lee visited here frequently while trying to develop a strategy for the lower coast in late 1861.

On occasion, reenactors fire a full-scale coastal defense cannon here; this is one of the few forts in the country that fires such a large gun.

Fort Pulaski

Fort Pulaski, now a National Monument, is about 15 miles east of Savannah on US 80; call 912-786-5787 for information.

Second Lieutenant Robert E. Lee arrived at Fort Pulaski on desolate Cockspur Island in November 1829, no doubt with second thoughts about the glamour of the Engineer Corps. There was nothing glamorous about the mosquitoes, water moccasins, and alligators he discovered here. Lee was so bored that he found time to draw pictures of creatures such as turtles and alligators.

Among the senior officers who served at Cockspur Island with Lee was Lieutenant Joseph K. F. Mansfield, who was four years older than Lee but seven years ahead at West Point, since he had entered when he was only 13.

Lee served less than six months at Cockspur Island, leaving well before the fort was finished, but his engineering work can still be seen. Walk to the top of the parapets and look to all sides. The drainage ditches leading away from the fort are of Lee's design. For his part, Lieutenant Mansfield was so good at designing the fort's

Lee served less than six months at Cockspur Island, leaving before Fort Pulaski was finished.

foundation that park rangers say it has not settled one bit since it was finished in the mid-1840s. Lee left when he was transferred to do maintenance work on Fort Monroe in Norfolk, Virginia; his proximity to Arlington subsequently allowed him to propose to his childhood sweetheart, Mary Custis.

Lee again saw his first posting in early 1862, when he was sent by Jefferson Davis to assess the lower South's ability to withstand Union invasion. It was not a plum assignment. One of the reasons Lee was dispatched to Savannah was because he had lost the two campaigns in western Virginia with which he had been charged. Davis, irritated with the early losses at Cheat Mountain and Sewell Mountain, had no use for Lee in the field, so he shifted him to an advisory role.

Lee looked at Fort Pulaski and at Tybee Island, located about a mile farther east on the Atlantic Ocean. He decided to evacuate Tybee Island without a fight. He reasoned—as any military engineer trained in the early 1800s would have—that Fort Pulaski would prove a formidable opponent to any Union force trying to come up the Savannah River after landing on Tybee. There were no trees around the fort, so a land attack would be suicidal. Any ships heading up the river would be sunk before getting close. Even if a few cannon shells could make the mile distance, their force would be spent; they might even bounce

Lee designed the drainage ditches that lead away from Fort Pulaski.

off the fort's thick brick walls. Fort Pulaski was impregnable.

What Lee did not count on (and may not have known about before the Federals attacked on April 11, 1862) were the advances that had taken place in heavy artillery over the preceding two decades. The new heavy cannons flowing out of Northern foundries were rifled. When the 30-pound shells fired from such cannons began to rain down on Fort Pulaski, they burrowed deep within the brick walls before exploding. It took only a few hours before the fort's eastern wall was smashed. A lucky cannon shot now had a direct line toward the fort's magazine. The Confederates surrendered rather than be blown to bits.

Lee was shocked at how quickly the fort had fallen, and how. In a sense, his whole career must have passed in front of him. He had scouted locations for forts in Florida, designed the drainage for Fort Pulaski in Georgia, strengthened Fort Monroe in Virginia, repaired Fort Hamilton in New York, and totally designed Fort Carroll in Maryland. Now, all of those forts were instantly obsolete, subject to being blown to the ground by a few well-paced cannon shells.

Could Lee have stopped the Federals from landing on Tybee Island and thereby saved Fort Pulaski? It is doubtful. He did not have an army with him. All of the heavy guns were at Fort Pulaski and Fort Jackson. He may have slowed the Federal advance some, but the same overwhelming force that landed at Tybee would eventually have landed anyway.

Still, in Davis's mind, and in the minds of newspaper editors as well, Lee had failed in yet another campaign. The Confederacy was beginning to lose faith in the man who had proven unable to save western Virginia, southern South Carolina, and coastal Georgia from Union invasion. It would be another six months—June 1862—before Lee would successfully defend Richmond and change all of the minds.

As for Joseph K. F. Mansfield, the man who had the most to do with the design of Fort Pulaski, he made a career in the army, just like Lee. He, too, served in the Mexican War. In September 1862, he fell dead leading his men in a Union charge at Sharpsburg against an army headed by his old subordinate, Lee.

Cumberland Island

This 17-mile-long barrier island, located on the border between Georgia and Florida, may be reached by boats from Fernandina Beach, Florida, and St. Marys, Georgia. It is now a National Seashore; only 300 people per day are allowed to visit. The grave of Light Horse Harry Lee is located in the old family cemetery beside the ruins of Dungeness, the second home of that name to occupy the site. Dungeness is reached by an easy walk from the ferry dock. Call 912-882-4335 for reservations on the tour boat that leaves daily from St. Marys except on Christmas. No provisions are available on the island, so bring your own.

Cumberland Island has been occupied by humans for 4,000 years. Today, it is where sea turtles go to lay eggs and where sun worshipers go to get away from civilization. It is also where Robert E. Lee came on at least two occasions to visit the grave of his father.

Revolutionary War general Henry "Light Horse Harry" Lee, so nicknamed because of his mastery of cavalry forces, never officially lived on Cumberland Island. He just put ashore here to die.

The elder Lee lived (and avoided his creditors) in the West Indies for nearly five years before his death. Finally, homesickness and real sickness drove him on a journey to return to Virginia. He never made it. In March 1818, his ship pulled ashore at Cumberland Island, and Lee was taken to Dungeness. Perhaps by pure chance, Dungeness was the home of the daughter of Lee's old commander, General Nathanael Greene. Lee lived in the house for about two weeks. He died at age 62 and was buried in a small family cemetery on the island. Robert was 11 at the time.

Lee visited his father's grave at least twice, in 1862 and 1870. Some historians have speculated that he likely made his first trip in 1829, when he was briefly stationed at nearby Cockspur Island outside Savannah to help engineer the construction of Fort Pulaski. During his January 1862 trip, Lee combined family and military business, as he was also inspecting a Confederate battery on the extreme south side of the island, pointing toward the St. Marys River. Accounts say that Lee was silent during the few minutes he took to visit the Greene family cemetery. When Lee again stopped at Dungeness in 1870, his daughter Agnes decorated her grandfather's grave with flowers. Lee wrote of the grave, "I presume it is the last time I shall be able to pay it my tribute of respect."

Henry Lee's remains were removed from the grave in 1913 and taken to Lexington, Virginia, to rest with the other members of the Lee family.

Fort Pickens/Fort DeSoto/ Fort Zachary Taylor/Fort Jefferson/ Fort Clinch

All of these brick forts still exist and are open to the public. Fort Pickens is on West Santa Rosa Island near Pensacola; call 850-934-2600 for information. Fort DeSoto is off I-275 near St. Petersburg; call 727-866-2484. Fort Zachary Taylor is in Key West; call 305-292-6713. Fort Jefferson, the largest fort in the United States, is reachable only by seaplane or boat, as it lies 70 miles west of Key West in the Dry Tortugas; call 305-242-7700. Fort Clinch, at Fernandina Beach, now serves as a Florida State Park; call 904-277-7274.

Robert E. Lee visited Florida in early 1846 for a fairly lengthy examination of the coastal defenses from Pensacola to Fernandina Beach, as part of the effort to erect a string of forts around the country. Though it is known that he examined Forts Pickens, DeSoto, Zachary Taylor,

During his Southern tour in 1870, Lee visited a former colonel who lived on a plantation on the St. Johns River.

Jefferson, and Clinch, few historical details of the trip remain.

Lee subsequently angered Florida's Confederate officials in February 1862, when he was in Savannah as commander of the Department of South Carolina, Georgia, and Florida. After reading reports about how easily all of the Florida forts could be captured and how difficult it would be to protect the state's vast coastline from invasion, he suggested to President Jefferson Davis that Florida be abandoned. Davis followed that advice and sent the bulk of Florida's troops to the Army of Tennessee and what would become the Army of Northern Virginia, which would be commanded by Lee beginning four months later. Lee apparently never visited the state during the war.

The next time Lee was in Florida was in 1870, when he played the role of an old tourist. He landed in Jacksonville from a ship coming down from Savannah, Georgia. So many people crowded on the boat to get a chance to see Lee that the captain feared the vessel would sink under their weight. He persuaded Lee to go up on deck so the people on shore would have no need to try to board. When Lee appeared, a hush fell over the crowd. A local newspaper wrote that the silence "spoke a deeper feeling than the loudest huzzas could have expressed."

Lee left within a half-hour on the boat to visit a former colonel who lived on a plantation near Palatka, a small town on US 17 on the St. Johns River about 35 miles east of Gainesville. Lee and daughter Agnes spent the night at the plantation. According to reports, Lee delighted in walking out the front door of the house and picking his own oranges—something many a Florida orange farmer has had to endure from many a Florida tourist in the 130-plus years since Lee visited. Reports also say Lee spent time on the riverbank fishing—another favorite Florida tourist activity. Lee's visit to Palatka is not covered by any historical marker.

Jefferson Barracks

I-70, I-64, I-55, and I-44 converge at St. Louis. The house where Lee and his family lived no longer stands. Jefferson Barracks County Park is at the end of South Broadway Street about 10 miles south of downtown St. Louis in the community of Lemay. It is open Tuesday through Sunday. Call 314-544-5714 for information.

St. Louis would be nothing like it is today if not for Robert E. Lee. No, Lee never came near the Union city during the Civil War, so it didn't experience his guns. It was 35 years before the war when Lee visited St. Louis as a civil engineer. It is not unreasonable to say that the entire city survives because of him.

In 1836, it was becoming painfully obvious to the citizens of the growing city of St. Louis that the Mississippi River was out of control—meaning that it was not doing what would benefit the city's merchants. As rivers are wont to do, the Mississippi was changing course. It was slowly but surely moving east, cutting a new channel for itself closer to Illinois. Within a year or two, St. Louis would be a river town cut off from its river. Within a decade or two, it would be landlocked.

The town fathers appealed to Washington for an army engineer—armed with a congressional appropriation—to solve the problem. Lee drew the assignment. What he accomplished was a pioneering example of what the United States Army Corps of Engineers now does on a regular basis—direct water flow.

Arriving in St. Louis in August 1837 with a young assistant, Lieutenant Montgomery Meigs (who in 1864 would turn Lee's Arlington Plantation into a military cemetery), Lee explored the Mississippi as far north as Des Moines, Iowa, to try to get an understanding of the flow of the water. At first, he was not impressed with St. Louis. In fact, he called it "the dirtiest place I was ever in."

The engineering problem Lee faced was simple. Over the years, the river's eastward movement had allowed silt to accumulate on the Missouri side, creating two islands above and below St. Louis—Bloody Island and Duncan's Island. Both islands—really very large sand bars—were slowly growing in size and creeping toward St. Louis, threatening to fill in completely.

The solution was equally simple, in theory. Lee's job was to divert the river back toward Missouri, scouring the two islands away and making sure the shipping lanes ran close by the city. He thus needed to design a series of rock dykes across the Illinois side of the river in order to divert the flow back toward St. Louis.

Lee worked on the project for nearly three years. During the third year, Congress pulled the appropriation, forcing Lee to come home. He was promoted to captain in recognition of his service. Understanding the need to continue the work, the city of St. Louis appointed an engineer suggested by Lee to complete the project.

Decades after Lee's death, the mayor of St. Louis had this to say: "By his rich gift of genius and scientific knowledge, Lt. Lee brought the Father of Waters under control." At one time, the city considered putting up a statue of Lee.

There is no evidence of the islands that once attracted the attention of a future Confederate general. But it is the absence of those islands that proves his work. There seems little doubt that St. Louis would never have become what it is today without the service of Lee.

Lieutenant Colonel Lee briefly served at Jefferson Barracks in 1855, after taking the position of executive officer of the Second United States Cavalry Regiment following his service at West Point. The Second turned out to be a who's who of the Civil War. In its ranks were Albert Sidney Johnston, William J. Hardee, Earl Van Dorn, and Edmund Kirby-Smith (who would all become Confederate generals), as well as George Stoneman and George H. Thomas (who would become Union generals).

Lee was senior officer at Jefferson Barracks, but his service was tedious and frustrating. The regiment had been formed so quickly that some new men had not even been issued uniforms. When he found one man reporting for duty in dirty, tattered pants and an undershirt, Lee demanded to know why he was not in uniform. The soldier replied that was all he had. Lee ordered him down to the Mississippi to wash and mend his clothes.

Lee spent only a few months here before starting a round of court-martial duty that took him virtually all over the country, from Texas to Pennsylvania.

Camp Cooper

This camp lay about 12 miles southwest of the town of Throckmorton, which is located at the junction of US 283 and US 380 southwest of Wichita Falls and northwest of Fort Worth. What remains of the camp is on private property, though there is a historical marker on RR 2528. To see the marker, drive 10 miles south from Throckmorton on US 283, turn right on RR 2584, drive about four miles, then turn left on RR 2528.

In 1857, Lee was assigned to Camp Cooper, his northernmost posting in Texas, from Fort Mason, located about 170 miles south. He relieved Major William J. Hardee, a future Confederate general. Camp Cooper was supposed to be in the middle of Comanche country, and it was the job of the Second United States Cavalry to keep an eye on the Indians. Lee met the local chief but did not think much of him or his six wives.

There was not much to Camp Cooper then or now. The men lived in tents, as there were no trees from which to construct houses. Lee made the most of his Spartan life at the camp. He somehow brought seven chickens with him for their egg-laying ability. He had to build a chicken coop off the ground in order to protect the birds from the abundant rattlesnakes in the area. In one letter home, Lee even claimed to have made a pet of a rattlesnake.

Lee led a 40-day ride of the Second Cavalry around west Texas looking for renegade Comanches but failed to find a single one. Another detachment fought a brief battle, killing two Indians. Lee reached the conclusion that there were very few hostile Indians to fight in that part of Texas.

Fort Mason

The town of Mason is located about 100 miles northwest of San Antonio at the junction of US 87, US 377, and TX 29. The reconstructed officers' quarters are all that remain of Fort Mason today. Visitors can find them at 110 Spruce Street, in the southern part of town about three blocks south of Court House Square off Post Hill Street.

It was in March 1856—exactly 10 years after his first assignment in Texas—when Lee returned to the state. He was second-in-command of the Second United States Cavalry. He was actually given his cavalry assignment in April 1855, but almost immediately after getting those orders, he was issued other orders to go all over the country on court-martial duty. The Second Cavalry went to Texas without him.

Lee caught up to his men the next year, after passing through the military headquarters town of San Antonio. His first duty posting was to Fort Mason, in what is now the town of Mason. His primary duty was fighting Indians, but if he even saw a hostile, much less shot at one, it never made it into his official reports. One officer who did shoot at Indians was Lieutenant John Bell Hood, later one of Lee's generals.

Lee left Texas to return to Arlington to settle his father-in-law's estate. It took nearly three years. He was back in Texas in 1860. As fall and winter approached, the newspapers were filled with talk of the South's leaving the Union. Lee wrote a flurry of letters from Texas blaming the crisis on the cotton states of the Deep South, like South Carolina and Alabama, and the abolitionists of the North. In one letter, he wrote that "one of [the Southern firebrands'] plans seems to be the renewal of the slave trade. That I am opposed to on every ground."

Back at Fort Mason in January 1861, Lee wrote, "I can anticipate no greater calamity for the country than a dissolution of the Union. It would be an accumulation of all the evils we complain of, and I am willing to sacrifice everything but honor for its preservation."

In early February, Lee received a strange order from his commander, General Winfield Scott, asking him to come immediately to Washington. On February 13, he left Fort Mason for a meeting with Scott during which Lee was promoted to full colonel—and during which he may have been offered command of the Northern armies, though that will never be known for certain. That meeting took place three days before Abraham Lincoln's inauguration.

When Fort Mason was closed in 1869, the citizens living nearby dismantled many of the stone buildings and used the materials in their own homes. All that remains of the fort today is a reconstructed officers' quarters maintained by the Mason County Historical Society.

San Antonio

The principal access routes to this south Texas city are I-35, I-37, I-10, US 90, US 181, and US 281. The Vance Hotel (now the Camberly Gunther Hotel), located at 205 East Houston Street, was the headquarters of the Second United States Cavalry.

Lee first arrived in San Antonio in September 1846 with the unglamourous job of gathering the picks and shovels that would be needed to build roads and bridges once the United States Army invaded Mexico. He was in town just a week before leaving for Mexico. It was from San Antonio that Captain Lee, 38 years old and 17 years in the army, rode out in his first military column. Up to that point in his career, the future general who would one day command 90,000 men had been a solitary engineer in charge of only himself. He had rarely camped out in the open. Suddenly, he was part of a large army.

In July 1857, during his second tour in Texas, Lee was ordered from Camp Cooper to San Antonio to take command of the Second United States Cavalry when its colonel, Albert Sidney Johnston, was ordered to Washington. Lee was there only four months before his father-in-law died in Arlington, after which he secured a leave of absence from the army to handle family affairs. At that point, he had served in Texas from the wilds of Camp Cooper to the comfort of San Antonio for 19 months.

After putting those affairs in order, Lee went back to Texas. In February 1861, he was at Fort Mason when he received the communication from General Winfield Scott directing him to come to Washington. Lee's path to the nation's capital led through San Antonio. When he arrived at the Second Cavalry's headquarters at the Vance

Hotel on February 16, he was shocked to discover that General David Twiggs, a Southern sympathizer and the commander of United States forces in Texas, had already surrendered those forces and all United States property within Texas. In effect, United States lieutenant colonel Robert E. Lee was a prisoner in a war yet to be declared.

An angry Lee refused to deal with the secessionists. He prudently decided to dress in civilian clothes as he made plans to get to Washington. Lee was so dispirited at the situation that he told his friends he planned to resign from the army and "go to planting corn." He left his baggage in the care of a friend in San Antonio and rushed to the coast to catch a steamer for Washington. He was afraid that the secessionists would arrest him, as they did other United States officers who stumbled into the same situation. When Lee left Indianola, Texas, on February 22, 1861, it was the last time he was in the state.

Though Texas secessionists angered Lee before the war started, Texas troops proved extremely loyal to him once the fighting began.

Rio Grande City

This town is located on the Rio Grande about 110 miles upriver from the Gulf of Mexico. US 83 gives access to Rio Grande City from the east and the northwest and TX 755 from the northeast. The Lee House is one of the Rio Grande Consolidated School District buildings, located on the Fort Ringgold Campus on US 83 East in the downtown area.

During his 1856-57 tour of duty in Texas, Lee spent seven months at Fort Brown (today's Brownsville), located on the Rio Grande about 90 miles east of Rio Grande City. His time there was a tedious round of court-martial duty. It was while at Fort Brown that Lee wrote a lengthy letter to his wife predicting that efforts by "certain people of the North to interfere with and change the domestic institutions of the South" would lead to "civil and servile war." Lee wrote about slavery in the letter, calling it "a moral and political evil in any country." He gave his opinion that black people were much better off in the United States than in Africa and that "the melting influence" of white and black Christians would eventually lead to their emancipation. No Lee sites remain in Brownsville today.

When Lee returned to Texas in February 1860 after putting his family affairs back in order following the death of his father-in-law, his major duty was to ride to Ringgold Barracks at Rio Grande City to protect Texas citizens from the activities of the bandit Juan Cortina. Unable to find the bandit, Lee returned to San Antonio, then went back to Fort Mason. He lived at the Lee House while in Rio Grande City investigating Cortina.

Bibliography

Brooks, Robert B. "Robert E. Lee: Civil Engineer." *Civil Engineering* (March 1940):167-69.

Civil War Book of Lists, The. Conshohocken, PA: Combined Books, 1993.

Crute, Joseph H., Jr. *Derwent: Robert E. Lee's Sanctuary*. Midlothian, VA: Derwent Books, 1995.

Davis, Burke. *Gray Fox: Robert E. Lee and the Civil War*. Short Hills, NJ: Burford Books, 1956.

Davis, Charles G. "Camp Cooper." *The Handbook of Texas Online*. February 15, 1999. http://www.tsha.utexas.edu/handbook/online/articles/view/CC/qbc9.html.

DeVos, Julius E. "Fort Mason." *The Handbook of Texas Online*. February 15, 1999. http://www.tsha.utexas.edu/handbook/online/articles/view/FF/qbf34.html.

Eicher, David J. *Robert E. Lee: A Life Portrait*. Dallas, TX: Taylor Publishing Company, 1997.

Freeman, Douglas Southall. *R. E. Lee: A Biography*. New York: Charles Scribner's Sons, 1934.

Hennessy, John J. *Return to Bull Run*. New York: Simon and Schuster, 1993.

Johnson, Clint. *Touring the Carolinas' Civil War Sites*. Winston-Salem, NC: John F. Blair, Publisher, 1996.

————. *Touring Virginia's and West Virginia's Civil War Sites*. Winston-Salem, NC: John F. Blair, Publisher, 1999.

Lee, Richard M. *General Lee's City*. McLean, VA: EPM Publications, 1987.

Lee, Robert E., Jr. *Recollections and Letters of General Robert E. Lee*. Garden City, NY: Garden City Publishing, 1904.

Meredith, Roy. *The Faces of Robert E. Lee*. New York: Charles Scribner's Sons, 1947.

Moore, Samuel J. T., Jr. *Moore's Complete Civil War Guide to Richmond*. Richmond, VA: self-published, 1978.

Salmon, John S., comp. *A Guidebook to Virginia's Historical Markers*. Charlottesville, VA: University Press of Virginia, 1994.

Sanborn, Margaret. *Robert E. Lee: A Portrait*. Moose, WY: Homestead Publishing, 1966.

Soderberg, Susan Cooke. *A Guide to Civil War Sites in Maryland*. Shippensburg, PA: White Mane Books, 1998.

Taylor, John M. *Duty Faithfully Performed*. Dullas, VA: Brassy's, 1999.

Thomas, Emory M. *Robert E. Lee: An Album*. New York: W. W. Norton and Company, 2000.

Wert, Jeffrey D. *General James Longstreet*. New York: Simon and Schuster, 1993.

Index

United States Marines, 107, 108
United States Military Academy
(West Point), 1, 85, 93,
121-24
United States Military Academy
Museum, 121

Valley Mountain, W.Va., 112
Vance Hotel, 174
Van Dorn, Earl, 169
Vermont. *See* Glenaire
Violet Bank, 67-68
Virginia, 1-99
Virginia Capitol, 52
Virginia Central Railroad, 76
Virginia troops, 21, 138

Warm Springs, Va., 91
Warrenton, N.C., 144
Warrenton Turnpike, 39
Washington College, 79, 93, 96,
144
Washington, D.C., 101-4
Washington Hall, 96
Washington & Lee University, 93,
121
Washington, George, 5, 25, 26,
27, 34, 63

Washington, John Augustine, 114
Washington, Lewis, 108
Washington, Martha, 63
Weed, Stephen, 123
West, Benjamin, 59
West Point, Va., 60-61
West Virginia, 105-20
West Woods, 140, 142
Wheat Field, The, 134
White House, The, 89, 104
White House Plantation, Va.,
63-64
White Marsh, 60, 61, 62, 65
White Sulphur Letter, 120
White Sulphur Springs, W.Va.,
117-20
White's Ford, Va., 109
Widow Tapp Farm, 18-19
Wilderness, The, 13, 16, 18-20,
45, 76, 86
Williams, Seth, 85, 90
Wilmington, N.C., 145, 146
Wise, Henry, 110, 115, 116

York River, 61